Burgess Sport Teaching Series

TEACHING SOCCER

William Thomson

Technical Director
Canadian Soccer Association

Original illustrations by
George Marjanovic

Burgess Publishing Company
Minneapolis, Minnesota

Consulting Editor: Robert D. Clayton, Colorado State University

Editorial: Wayne Schotanus, Marta Reynolds
Art: Joan Gordon, Adelaide Trettel
Production: Morris Lundin, Pat Barnes
Composition: Jeanette Baynes

Cover design: Adelaide Trettel

Burgess Publishing Company
7108 Ohms Lane
Minneapolis, Minnesota 55435

Contents

Acknowledgments   vi
Diagram Symbols   vii

1 Introduction   1

2 Teaching Methods   2
　　Organization   2
　　Assessment   3
　　Instruction   4

3 Teaching Objectives   6
　　Development of Behavioral Objectives   6
　　Lesson Planning   8
　　Suggested Projects   14

4 Organization   15
　　Coeducational Grouping   15
　　Facilities   15
　　Class Formations   17
　　Equipment   19
　　Individual Equipment   22
　　Suggested Projects   23

5 Level 1 Teaching Progressions   24
　　Passing Techniques   24
　　Passing Practice   26
　　Receiving and Ball Control Techniques   29
　　Receiving and Ball Control Practice   31
　　Techniques for Running with the Ball   33
　　Running with the Ball Practice   34

Tackling Technique   35
Tackling Practice   37
Kicking and Shooting Technique   38
Kicking and Shooting Practice   39
Goalkeeping Techniques   41
Goalkeeping Practice   43
Heading Techniques   44
Heading Practice   45
Passing and Shooting Skill Practice   47
Goalkeeping Skill Practice   50
Dribbling Skill Practice   50
Tackling Skill Practice   51
Shooting Skill Practice   51
Receiving Skill Practice   52
Heading Skill Practice   53
Small-Sided Games   56

6   Level 2 Teaching Progressions   58
Warmup Games   58
Techniques for Lifting the Ball   61
Practice Lifting the Ball   63
Techniques for Striking the Bouncing Ball   64
Volleying Practice   65
Receiving Techniques   66
Receiving Practice   67
Dribbling Techniques   68
Tackling Techniques   69
Dribbling and Tackling Practice   70
Goalkeeping Techniques   71
Goalkeeping Practice   77
Heading Technique   78
Heading Practice   79
Receiving Skill Practice   79
Passing Skill Practice   82
Heading Skill Practice   84
Tackling and Dribbling Skill Practice   85
Goalkeeping Skill Practice   88
Game-Related Practices   88
Small-Sided Games   89
Restarts   92

7   Level 3 Teaching Progressions   104
Functional Training   104
Systems of Play   110
Principles of Play   111
Coaching the Principles of Play   118

Methods of Conditioning   **133**
Endurance and Speed   **134**
Strength and Power   **144**
Agility/Mobility   **148**

8 Evaluation   **154**
Skills Award Program   **154**
Using the Evaluation Charts   **157**
Level 1 Test on Basic Soccer Rules   **164**

Appendix A: Recommendation for Mini Soccer 7 Aside Rules   **165**
Appendix B: Basic Rules of Soccer   **167**
Appendix C: Annotated Bibliography   **173**

Index   **175**

Acknowledgments

In my capacity as technical director of the Canadian Soccer Association over the past ten years, I have been fortunate in having the opportunity to compile and utilize a variety of coaching materials. This book is a collection of many of the drills and games presently used in our coaching program, and I am grateful both to the individuals who have assisted me in this endeavor and to the Canadian Soccer Association, which has permitted the reproduction and use of many of the materials published in their coaching material.

The editorial assistance of Prof. Robert Clayton of the University of Colorado and Marta Reynolds and Marcia Bottoms of Burgess Publishing Company was both necessary and much appreciated. George Marjanovic was responsible for the illustrations, and I am grateful for his artistic talent and knowledge of soccer, which made this text more explicit.

Diagram Symbols

G	Goalkeeper
RB	Right Fullback
LB	Left Fullback
RH	Right Halfback
CH	Center Halfback
LH	Left Halfback
OR	Outside Right
IR	Inside Right
CF	Center Forward
IL	Inside Left
OL	Outside Left

1

Introduction

Interest in soccer in North America has been exploding over the last few years, and the sport has become a popular activity that youngsters want to learn and teachers like to teach. The sport's rapidly increasing popularity has also created a demand for instructional books aimed at improving the skills of beginners.

Teaching Soccer concentrates on developing the skills and principles of the game of soccer at the same time it presents to the beginning coach, physical education major, or practicing teacher all the materials he or she will need in an organized system of instructional methods.

The presentation of most of the subjects taught in our schools and colleges has tended to be, quite naturally, one dependent on an educational philosophy. That is, the approach has been to present as much material about a sport as possible in the hope that the students would gain a broad knowledge of the skills and perhaps be able to apply some of their knowledge to the game. Of course, this approach has a great deal of merit in the introduction of ball skills to students at the youngest age levels when a familiarity and an awareness of motor ability is being developed. However, even at this elementary level of involvement, there tends to be no objective other than simple experimentation. Teachers at every level should set behavioral objectives that reflect the outcome expected in such involvement, and they should develop tasks that work toward the objectives or evaluate the behavior resulting from the objectives. In short, the premise upon which the material in this text is presented is that a systematic *task* approach is necessary for developing and evaluating soccer skills.

This text tries to give the teacher-coach a comprehensive reference of the methodology related to the coaching tasks associated with the game of soccer. The text is designed to help develop the competency of teachers and coaches so that they can select from the text the material appropriate for their students and incorporate it into a sound teaching program. A sound teaching program demands the organization of students, the analysis of performance, and the use of appropriate instructional techniques that allow evaluative feedback.

Throughout *Teaching Soccer,* the actual act of teaching by the instructor or coach will be emphasized to make important points. By approaching the teaching of soccer in this way, teaching can be just as much an art as it is a science.

2

Teaching Methods

Many teachers and coaches find that they are forced to introduce the game of soccer within a limited period of time, and, as a result, they are faced with the problem of achieving optimum development as efficiently as possible. This problem comes up in academic institutions at all levels when only a limited number of class periods are allotted to activities such as soccer. Each teacher has to decide whether to spend the class's time practicing basic skills or practicing the game itself.

Soccer is a game relatively new to the United States, and children and athletes are unfamiliar with the skills and patterns of play involved. In North America, the games that have been popular until now—hockey, softball, lacrosse, basketball, tennis, squash, badminton, and even football—all depend primarily on hand and eye coordination. Just as the Europeans have concentrated on soccer to the comparative exclusion of other games, we have neglected the coordination skills used in soccer in favor of those used in other sports. In most of our games, the feet and the lower limbs in general have been used only for locomotion, power, direction, and positioning after or during the execution of another skill. Of course, the limbs are used this way in soccer, too, but the important distinction is that in soccer for the first time we are introducing a factor of control, or *skill,* in the use of the lower limbs.

When coaching or introducing any skill, a teacher or a coach must consider a number of points. These points can be grouped generally under *organization, assessment,* and *instruction.*

ORGANIZATION

In the usual school situation, the physical education teacher attempting to teach soccer in a fall or a spring term is fortunate to have ten or fifteen sessions to devote to the task. Often, difficulties with the facilities available and the number of students in the class encroach on teaching time, and the teacher-coach is forced to organize a program that takes all the limiting factors into account.

The age group and level of skill of the players are other factors that the teacher-coach has to consider in developing a soccer program. For older age groups and even for semi-professional players who practice only once or twice a week, conditioning should be stressed and skill practice should take the form of a modified game. This approach is sound since the major weakness in soccer players is often a lack of fitness, but the means to this end are sometimes unrealistic and counterproductive. For example, calisthenics, or Swedish drill, are often badly used and even harmful. Fitness can be maintained through exercises with balls. Especially with young players, practice time is best spent on game skills and small-sided games and drills that stress skills while they produce as much variety and interest as possible. Formal conditioning can be omitted for the young players since skill practice gives enough conditioning for this age group.

Teachers and coaches often face large groups, limited facilities, and shortages of equipment. The physical education teacher especially often faces as many as forty students in a confined gymnasium or a soccer field with only enough equipment to give one ball to every two students.

Whether the teacher is faced with training on a gymnasium floor, a playground, a parking lot, or a field, the approach should be the same. First, he or she should assess the space available in comparison to the number of players in the class. Second, he or she should arrange the class so that everyone is able to see and hear the instruction. Formations in the practice area should vary with the number of players, the space available, and the type of practice.

Most teaching situations can be organized so that each student gets enough practice and the maximum amount of contact with the ball when these two organizational concepts are followed.

1. Divide the group into practice groups of four.
2. Use practice areas bounded by lines, cones, or other markings that will contain the groups of players.

Figure 2-1 illustrates examples of effective organization. The coaching grid (figure 2-1A) shown provides an area for four players practicing passing with the inside of the foot with one ball in a 10-yard-square area. If nine grids were used in a class, thirty-six players could be easily involved and supervised. When convenient grids are not available, four players could be arranged for a shuttle relay (figure 2-1B). Player number 1 advances with the ball to player number 2, who returns the ball to number 3, and so on.

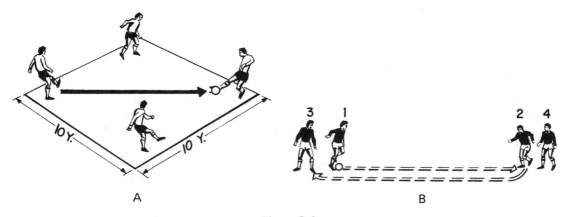

Figure 2-1

ASSESSMENT

The level of ability of the class or the team should be observed and assessed as early as possible in the teaching term. Otherwise, the teacher-coach may teach above or below the skill levels of the students. Assessment can be done during a short warmup game at the beginning of a session. The game can be either a regular game or a game adapted to focus on specific aspects of play. For example, if inaccurate passing turned out to be one of the class's major problems, the teacher could strive to correct it by giving the class practice in passing situations. Even when there is a prearranged lesson plan, a short game at the beginning of the session can still be valuable. Apart from the warmup effect, there is the opportunity for the teacher-coach to stop the play and illustrate a specific skill the moment a weakness shows up. Then, after the skill has been demonstrated outside the game situation, it can be put back into the game again and the teacher can check for improvement. In this way, practice becomes meaningful and important to the players rather than something they must do before they are allowed to play a game.

INSTRUCTION

The debate among educators over *skill teaching* and *technique teaching* in sports has been going on for many years. The difference in approach arises from a basic disagreement over what constitutes *skill* in a game. Technique teaching involves the teaching of fundamental techniques outside the game situation (for example, teaching the push pass in pairs), with no opposition during practice. Skill teaching is approached by setting up situations that involve opponents, supporting players, and a target (for example, passing practice with three players against one with a target of three consecutive passes).

These two approaches need not be mutually exclusive. The danger lies in using one approach exclusively—only teaching techniques or only using skill drills. The skill approach should not exclude technique practice; it should use it to improve final skill performance.

A skill practice allows the teacher the opportunity to consider the nature of the mistakes being made in play. When it is determined that the mistakes stem from a lack of fundamental ability, some time should be spent practicing the techniques involved. However, if the teacher concludes that the mistakes are in the decisions being made by the players and not in their technique, the players should be exposed to situations that challenge the execution of their playing ability. The opposition can be constrained by putting them at a distance from the player, giving him or her more time to make the correct decisions. Once the player is proficient, he or she can be exposed to unrestrained practice.

Effective instruction includes the following three phases.

1. *Presentation:* New facts, techniques, teaching points, and drills are presented to the class. For example: a demonstration of the technique of passing with the inside of the foot.
2. *Application:* A technique presented to the class is practiced by the students. For example: a shuttle relay formation with four-player teams positioned 10 yards apart.
3. *Feedback:* The students receive feedback (evaluation) on the accuracy or adequacy of their response. For example: the players practice until they achieve the desired response (seven good passes out of ten tries).

The teacher-coach must remember the basic principle that some feedback, based upon an already established behavioral objective, should be given to the students often. Comments such as a simple "well done" or "that's better, now try to make three passes," should be given to individual players during every session. Feedback can be informal evaluations of performance in drills or, at appropriate levels, it can be formal testing of the objectives that have been established for the skills.

The three-phase procedure in instruction should be a regular part of the teaching methodology, but the length of time devoted to each phase can vary. In general, the newer the technique and the younger the age group, the more frequently the same principles and techniques need to be presented, applied, and evaluated.

3

Teaching Objectives

An *objective* describes the desired outcome of a learning experience, that is, what a student is able to do as a result of a learning experience. After a teacher has decided what the desired *behavior* should be, he or she skillfully develops suitable *tasks* that will enable the student to meet that *behavioral objective*. In the past, before a system of using behavioral objectives was developed, a teacher often decided what the objective of a unit was to be and then made a subjective assessment of whether or not an individual student had improved his or her skills during the performance of the game itself. To base an evaluation solely on game performance, particularly during the early stages of skill learning, was grossly unfair since there are so many other factors involved in a game setting in addition to the simple execution of soccer techniques. Because the performance of a prescribed task allows for the necessary feedback and increased motivation, setting behavioral objectives and using tasks constitute a very effective method of soccer instruction. By measuring and observing the students' behavior, a teacher-coach is able to determine whether or not a skill or a concept or a principle has been learned.

DEVELOPMENT OF BEHAVIORAL OBJECTIVES

A review of the tasks that a soccer coach has to contend with should serve to reveal the areas of concern. *Psychomotor tasks* involve the physical performance of techniques and skills. For example: learning the technique of passing in unopposed situations. *Cognitive tasks* involve the processing of knowledge related to the game. For example: learning the basic rules of the game. And *affective tasks* concern the influence of emotional behavior on the participation of the players. For example: learning the philosophy of sportsmanship in soccer.

The task approach used in setting behavioral objectives and in teaching tasks is exemplified for soccer in table 3-1, which shows a good system for setting individual and group tasks.

The development of behavioral objectives for any subject area should begin with a list of the perceived tasks that a teacher has to consider. The tasks listed in table 3-2 have been identified for teaching soccer and form the basis of the teaching progressions discussed in chapters 5, 6, and 7.

TABLE 3-1
SAMPLE BEHAVIORAL OBJECTIVES
AND TEACHING TASKS

BEHAVIORAL OBJECTIVES	TEACHING TASKS
Psychomotor Student using inside of foot, passes a ball so that teammate can play it. **Level 1:** Over a 10-yard distance, student completes six out of ten passes through teammate's legs. **Level 2:** Inside a 10-yard grid, student passes to two other teammates (while one opponent tries to intercept) and makes six successful passes without the opposition intercepting ball. **Level 3:** In small-sided game, student successfully maintains possession and interpasses to obtain shot on goal.	**Level 1:** Through the tunnel—two teammates, 10 yards apart, attempt to pass ball with inside of foot through open legs of teammate. **Level 2:** Three players against one opponent interpass within 10-yard square. **Level 3:** Five aside soccer—team in possession attempts to interpass successfully and score goal on opponents.
Cognitive In a written test, student demonstrates knowledge of these basic rules of soccer by scoring 90 percent on a written quiz covering various aspects of the game. **Level 1:** Field markings, restarts. **Level 2:** Misconduct. **Level 3:** Offside.	Player (student) studies class handouts, understands class discussion, and applies knowledge in game situations. **Tasks:** (1) Out of class, student reviews concise handout on basic soccer laws. (2) In class, student completes short self-test and checks answers with key provided. (3) Teacher should give a short (2-5 minutes long) lecture-demonstration on (a) field markings, (b) restarts, (c) fouls and misconduct, and (d) offside. During daily sessions, teacher reinforces rule interpretations when the occasion arises in practice.
Affective In game play, student displays acceptable sportsmanship by not jeering when a superior team outplays a poorer team.	Player (student) understands class discussion and applies it in game situations. **Tasks:** Teacher discusses sportsmanship concepts in these situations. (a) Team ahead 10-0, eleventh goal scored, member of winning team loudly says, "This isn't too tough," as she trots back to starting position. (b) Team that is behind 10-0 has another goal scored against them. As player on winning team returns to position, opponent angrily kicks the ball toward him.

TABLE 3-2
TEACHING TASKS

1. Set objectives for:
   (a) The individual player.
   (b) The team.
   (c) The practice session.
   (d) The game.
   (e) The season.
2. Select skills and activities for students that are appropriate to the students' ages and levels of ability so that the following items are covered:
   (a) Passing.
   (b) Kicking and shooting.
   (c) Heading.
   (d) Dribbling and tackling.
   (e) Receiving and controlling.
   (f) Goalkeeping.
   (g) Team play.

3. Plan the practice by:
   (a) Organizing the practice on the basis of established objectives and appropriate skills.
   (b) Observing safety precautions.
4. Present the material by:
   (a) Arranging the instructional setting.
   (b) Presenting selected skills/principles/information.
   (c) Guiding application/practice of skills/principles.
   (d) Analyzing performance of psychomotor, cognitive, affective principles.
   (e) Giving feedback on performance.
   (f) Motivating students.
   (g) Reevaluating each lesson/practice so that steps a-f can be repeated effectively during subsequent class sessions.

LESSON PLANNING

In the lesson plan shown in table 3-4, the teaching principles of presentation, application, and feedback are integrated into the teaching framework of organization, assessment, and instruction (all of which were discussed in chapter 2). The content of an appropriate lesson should vary with the age group and level of ability, but the framework for lesson planning should always consider the following sequence.

1. *Warmup (Assessment):* The practice or game situation is organized so that the teacher can *observe ability* and *gauge instruction.* This can be done daily to measure the progress gained from earlier sessions or after two or three days of instruction.
2. *Technique Practice:* The *presentation* of simple practice drills and formations is followed by *application* by the students and concluded with relevant evaluation *(feedback).*
3. *Skill Practice:* The techniques learned are *applied* in simple gamelike situations.
4. *Small-Sided Game Practice:* A small-sided game is a miniature version of soccer in which the players play in various combinations (see pp. 17-19).
5. *Coached Game:* The application of skills is taught in a real game by stressing learned techniques or altering the game in such a way that a particular technique is emphasized.

The selection of objectives and the formation of tasks is an integral part of the process of lesson planning and should be considered in the framework exemplified in table 3-3.

An example of a lesson for improving the use of the inside of the foot for passing in a game with an intermediate-level group of students is shown in table 3-4.

TABLE 3-3
SAMPLE LESSON PLAN OUTLINE

OBJECTIVE	TASKS SET BY TEACHER	FEEDBACK
	Assessment	
	Technique Practice	
	Skill Practice	
	Small-Sided Game Practice	
	Coached Game	

TABLE 3-4

IMPROVING THE USE OF INSIDE OF FOOT PASSING IN GAME (INTERMEDIATES)

OBJECTIVES	TASKS SET BY TEACHER	FEEDBACK
Evaluate passing ability in a small-sided game.	**Assessment** Five to a side game stressing interpassing and moving to receive ball.	Make at least three consecutive passes before opposition intercepts.
Pass the ball over 10 yards to a teammate with the inside of the foot so that ball can be returned immediately.	**Technique Practice** 1. One player rebounding the ball off the wall from a distance of 5-10 yards, using various techniques, e.g., inside and outside of foot passes.	Make ten passes with inside of foot without stopping ball.*
	2. One player wall passing—running alongside a rebound wall, passing and receiving the ball with the inside and outside of foot.	
	3. Two players of equal ability practicing together on a rebound wall.	
	4. One player running around in a circle while another passes, using various methods.	Repeat ten times with inside of each foot and change over.*
	5. One player adjusting his or her position by moving in and out in order to vary the weight and method of passing over various distances.	Repeat ten times using each method and then change over.*

6. Player A passing from 5 yards, receiver B rebounding the ball with the inside of foot for teammate to receive at point C.

Repeat ten times using each method and then change over.*

7. Practicing shuttle runs in groups of four.
   a. Player A passing to B and following the ball, B passing to C as A takes place of B.

Repeat until ten passes (each player) are made without stopping the ball.*

   b. Ball being passed from position A to B while players are rotating through positions A, B, C, D.

Repeat until each player executes ten passes without stopping the ball.*

KEY

⬛▶ Path of the ball

⬜▶ Path of the player without the ball

⬜⃝▶ Path of the player with the ball

TABLE 3-4 (con't.)

OBJECTIVES	TASKS SET BY TEACHER	FEEDBACK
	c. Player passing and moving to a new position within a 10-yard square.	Repeat until ten passes (each player) are made without stopping the ball, with ball kept within the 10-yard area.*
Make six consecutive passes with the inside of foot before opponent can intercept.	**Skill Practice** 1. Three players keeping possession against one opponent by passing and moving within a 10-yard square. **Teaching Points** 1. Movement when not in possession of the ball being stressed to give more alternatives to player on the ball.	Make six consecutive passes with the inside of foot before opponent can intercept.*

		You naturally make a triangular formation.
	2. Positioning with less space and time but good support and passing angles. Player A can pass easily to position B or C.	
	3. Positioning with more space and time but poor passing angles. Defender could intercept pass to positions D or E.	Learn to move intelligently in order to give support to player with the ball.

Teaching Point
Player on ball points where teammates are needed for support.

Cross opponents' end line in possession of the ball.	**Small-Sided Game Practice** 1. Two against two in an area 10 × 20 yards, interpassing to cross opponents' end line with the ball.	Interpass and score.*
	2. Four versus four in area 20 × 20 yards, interpassing and stressing principle of support in attack.	Interpass and score.*
Interpass to advance the ball into opponents' goal area and shoot on goal.	**Coached Game** Five aside, stressing inside of foot passing.	Interpass and shoot on goal.*

*Observe performance and give relevant instructions.

SUGGESTED PROJECTS

1. Referring to the example of a psychomotor objective on p. 6, construct a logical lesson plan for the skill of heading as performed by a beginner. (Chapter 5, Level 1 Teaching Progressions, shows the appropriate tasks and feedback techniques for fulfilling this objective.)
2. Construct a lesson plan for a cognitive objective such as learning restart patterns. (See Level 2, chapter 6.)
3. Construct a lesson plan for an affective task such as sportsmanship in a situation in which there was a deliberate foul during the last minute of a tie game.
4. Interview a soccer teacher. Ask what skills are the most difficult to teach beginners and why. Ask the same questions about intermediates.

4

Organization

Organization and preparation are steps essential to teaching soccer because the nature of the game requires freedom of movement. But the freedom of movement must be controlled so that learning can take place. Whether the group being taught is large or small, these three preteaching procedures should be followed. They're common sensical and foolproof!

1. Assess the facilities available. How much space is there? Is the playing surface suitable for soccer? Are the markings on the playing surface appropriate for the practice?
2. Assess the equipment available. Will marker cones be needed? How many balls will be needed? Would training vests be useful?
3. Organize the lesson on the basis of the facilities and equipment available as well as according to objectives appropriate for the students to learn.

COEDUCATIONAL GROUPING

Soccer is a game that is enjoyed equally by boys and girls. Before they reach puberty, there is no reason why they can't participate in a coeducational learning and playing environment. If anything, the earlier physical maturation of females often gives them an advantage in size and strength. But, after they reach puberty, it is advisable to provide boys and girls with separate but equal opportunities to practice and compete.

FACILITIES

Although soccer is a game that requires space for play and practice, the students should never just be turned loose to practice all over the field. When that happens, the teacher does more jogging than teaching!

A teacher who is lucky enough to have access to a practice field has a valuable teaching tool. Next to the soccer balls, the space available for play and practice is the most important requirement for teaching soccer. However, many teachers don't have access to regular playing fields except for use during actual games. Still, the problem is not insurmountable. Even many professional teams train in parking lots, playgrounds, indoor gymnasiums, and smaller rooms with unobstructed floor space. Coaches working with youth soccer clubs usually have similar problems with rented facilities, including limitations on the facilities available and what they are allowed to do with the facilities they do have.

No matter where the class (or the soccer club) will be training, though, the lesson should be planned according to the space available and the number of students who will be using it. The class should be arranged to give everyone the best possible practice space and to provide the best possible teaching situation as well. Everyone should be able to see and hear the teacher when he or she gives demonstrations and instructions.

The class can be arranged in a number of different formations, depending on the number of students, the space available, and the type of practice to be done. The teacher should use the colored lines and markings on gymnasium floors or define outdoor areas by using flags, spare balls, shirts, or other extra equipment.

The playing field should be large enough for the players to be able to do what adult players would be able to do. For example, if an adult goalkeeper could kick past the halfway line on a field, the younger players should be able to do so, too.

Regular soccer facilities can be adapted for mini soccer. (See figure 4-1.) In a study done at the University of Alberta, Canada, calculations were made to determine the normal requirements for the size of the playing field, the size of the goal, and the size of the ball for various age groups. Table 4-1 lists the results of the study.

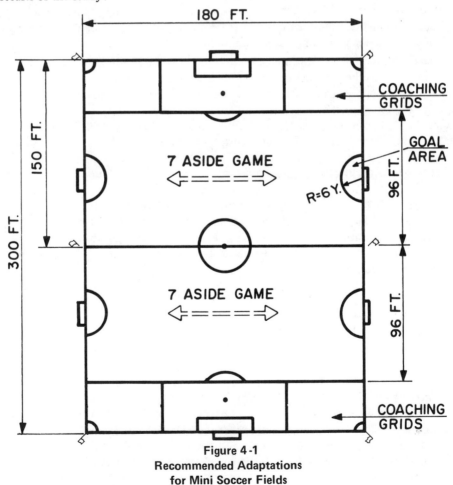

Figure 4-1
Recommended Adaptations
for Mini Soccer Fields

TABLE 4-1
EQUIPMENT AND FACILITIES REQUIRED
FOR VARIOUS AGE GROUPS

AGE	PLAYING FIELD		GOAL		BALL	
	Length	Width	Width	Height	Circumference	Size
8-10	80 yards	48 yards	18 feet	6 feet	21-22	2
10-12	85 yards	50 yards	18 feet	6 feet	23-24	3
12-14	100 yards	58 yards	21 feet	7 feet	25-26	4
14-16	105 yards	65 yards	24 feet	8 feet	27-28	5

SOURCE: Canadian Soccer Association *Mini Soccer Rules.*

CLASS FORMATIONS
Indoor Practice Areas

Formations that are useful in indoor practice areas are illustrated in figure 4-2. Figure 4-2A shows a warmup formation in which there is free dribbling with the ball. Circles or lines marked on the floor can be used as boundaries. A skill practice formation is shown in figure 4-2B. The gym is divided into practice grids marked with cones or lines. Various functional practices can be done at the same time in the formation illustrated in figure 4-2C.

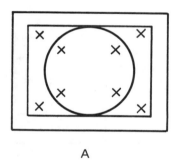
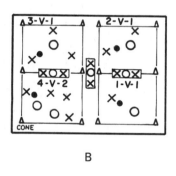
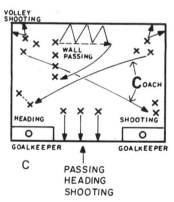

A	B	C

Figure 4-2

Indoor Games

Small-sided games are miniature versions of soccer in which two or more players play against an equal number of players in a small area. Even indoors, small-sided games allow the players a great deal of contact with the ball. In four-goal soccer (figure 4-3A), the flat top of a gym bench is used as a goal. Two players defend each goal and play together as a pair to attack the other goals when a goal has been scored against them and the scoring pair takes their place at the goal. Two-court soccer (figure 4-3B) is similar to crosscourt basketball. The gym is divided into two playing areas and four benches are used as goals. Indoor soccer (figure 4-3C) accommodates large groups. The group is divided into six teams, which play round robin or in a combined team competition.

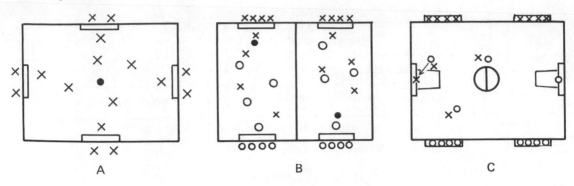

Figure 4-3

Outdoor Practice Areas

The area used for practice on an outdoor field should be limited. As much of the space as possible should be put to use, but, when the students are too far from the teacher, valuable teaching contact can be lost and the teacher's ability to teach and keep the class's interest may suffer. A warmup formation useful for outdoor practice is shown in figure 4-4A. The students can be confined in an area around the center or in the penalty box. For skill practice (figure 4-4B), the class can be confined to half of the field and a grid system with 10-yard squares can be set up for passing practice in small groups. A shooting drill (figure 4-4C) at one end of the field can involve many students at the same time in a functional practice.

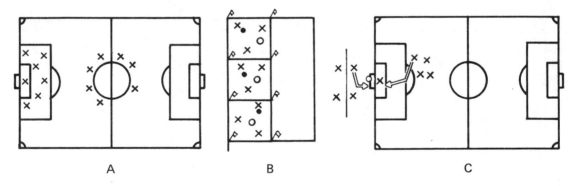

Figure 4-4

Outdoor Games

Small-sided team games can be used for large classes outdoors, with the play done across the field and flags, balls, or hockey goals used for targets on the sidelines (figure 4-5A). A goal for a small-sided game can be improvised on the halfway line, and the game can be played in each half (figure 4-5B).

The coaching grid is an excellent teaching aid for organizing skill practices and small-sided games. The grid is an area marked off in boxes 10 to 20 yards square. In addition to the markings and colored lines on gym floors and outdoor practice areas, flags, spare balls, shirts, and other equipment can be used to define the boundaries of the grid (see figure 4-6).

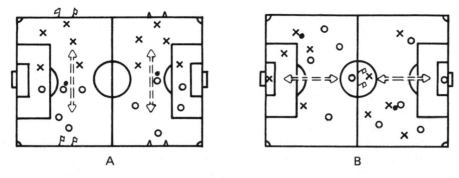

Figure 4-5

The Coaching Grid

The advantage of this type of organization include: (1) players have more contact with the ball in a small-sided game than they would playing in teams of eleven against eleven; (2) the coach has closer contact with the group in a confined area; (3) large numbers of players can be controlled more easily inside the grids; and (4) the size of the area and the size of the group can be varied in order to practice different aspects of the game.

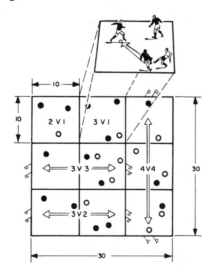

Figure 4-6

EQUIPMENT

One of the reasons that soccer has become so popular in North America recently is the low cost of its equipment compared to the cost of equipment for other sports, such as football. Even so, teachers and coaches often must deal with limited facilities and shortages of equipment. Physical education and athletics departments in schools sometimes have limited budgets, and soccer must compete with other sports for funds and space, as well as for time in the year's program. Independent youth soccer clubs, too, often have tight budgets since they depend on membership fees, proceeds from social fundraisers, and sponsors for their support.

Practice balls are probably the most important pieces of equipment for a basic soccer program. Particularly with beginners, having a suitable ball for each player provides for the best learning situation. (See table 4-1 for a list of the ball sizes appropriate for various ages.) One ball for every four players is the minimum that should be available. Instead of buying five first-class match balls for a class, it might be better in some situations to buy one match ball and invest the rest of the money allocated for balls in heavy-duty, imitation rubber (not plastic) playground balls. These balls are ideal for practicing a variety of skills and they don't lose their shape or gain weight when wet. Physical education teachers who teach other sports besides soccer may find it better to invest in general purpose practice balls instead of in a number of basketballs, volleyballs, and soccerballs.

Playing mini soccer on a regular field requires the use of mini goals. A child between seven and ten years old asked to defend the same goal area an adult would faces a frustrating, impossible task. This situation can have a negative effect on the individual player and on the quality of the whole game. A mini goal scaled down to the size of the players can be easily constructed (see figure 4-7). The collapsible and portable pieces of the goal include two triangular ends and two detachable lengths made of 2- to 3-inch plumbers of aluminum tubing that can be cut in various sizes for various age groups. Construction plans for the mini goal are available from the Canadian Soccer Association in the booklet *Mini Soccer Rules*. The British Columbia Juvenile Soccer Association has found crossbar lengths of 8, 10, and 12 feet to be appropriate for the ages six, seven, and eight, respectively. Obviously, a larger model could be made for older students. (See table 4-1 for a list of goal dimensions appropriate for various age groups.)

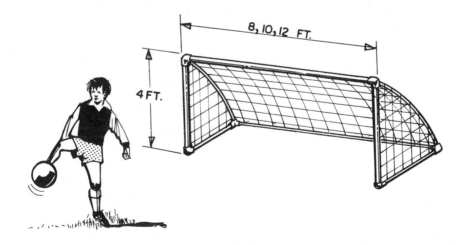

Figure 4-7
Mini Goal

Rebound Wall

A bang board or a rebound wall is an excellent aid for practicing shooting, passing, and kicking. The rebound wall (figure 4-8) can be a simple solid wooden fence or panel either the same size as a goal or smaller (to improve the player's aim). The rebound wall can be used by a player who throws the ball against the wall (or has a teammate make a throw-in) and lets it bounce once before driving it back with a half volley or a side volley. The player could also try to rebound the ball continuously by kicking the ball against the wall with half volley and side volley techniques.

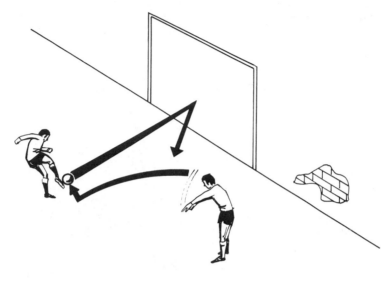

Figure 4-8

The rebound wall can also be marked off in sections (with painted lines) that indicate the desirable shooting zones (that is, the areas that are good to aim for). The player could run alongside a rebound wall, passing and receiving the ball with the inside or the outside of the foot. A shot on goal could be made at the end of the run (see figure 4-9).

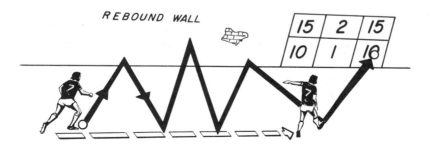

Figure 4-9

Pendulum Ball

The pendulum ball is a more sophisticated piece of practice equipment that can be used for specific skills. The pendulum ball is simply a tether ball suspended by a length of cord. The ball can be attached to a crossbar for practice with heading contacts. The height of the ball should be adjusted until contact can be made flat on the player's forehead when he or she has his or her feet flat on the ground (figure 4-10A). The ball can be suspended closer to the ground for practice in foot positioning for shooting and passing. The ball should rest on the ground with the rope tight for a consistent return after striking (figure 4-10B). The length of the swing and the speed of the return can be adjusted by holding the rope at various heights for practicing a variety of contacts (for example, volleys).

A   B

Figure 4-10

INDIVIDUAL EQUIPMENT

Students in a ten- or fifteen-week soccer unit won't require special uniforms or shoes. Running shoes are adequate, and regular gym shorts and shirts are comfortable for playing soccer.

However, in an organized competitive soccer program or in a youth soccer league, the players probably should invest in low-cost soccer shoes with leather uppers and rubber, multistud, molded soles. They should also have built-in arch supports and heel supports. There are a variety of brands on the market. More advanced players may also want to stretch their budgets for an additional pair of shoes with detachable screw-in studs, which are more suitable than rubber-studded shoes for wet-weather games. In any case, the shoes should fit snugly. Loose shoes cause blisters.

Traditional soccer socks are knee-high hose tied just below the knees with bandage tape or laces. The socks probably were worn originally so that the players could wear shin guards under them.

This piece of equipment is often overlooked by modern soccer players, but it's an important protection for the lower legs, especially for young soccer players. It is both painful and dangerous for a child to suffer injuries to the tibia bone during his or her growing years. Older players might also consider how tired their legs become after repeated contacts in the lower legs. Short soccer shorts are the traditional uniform. They should be loose fitting to allow for a maximum range of motion. There are a number of styles of shirts, but, again, it is most important that they are loose fitting and comfortable.

SUGGESTED PROJECTS

1. Prepare a diagram of a field suitable for seven to ten year olds. Indicate an ideal practice/playing arrangement.
2. Diagram the existing indoor and outdoor spaces at a school with which you are familiar. Divide the areas into logical playing areas for ten to twelve year olds, twelve to fourteen year olds, and other age groups.
3. Diagram the existing indoor and outdoor facilities of a school, and evaluate the facilities as areas for practicing passing, heading, etc., with a whole class working at the same time.
4. Diagram an existing indoor and outdoor facility, and divide the areas into as many coaching grids as are safely possible.

5

Level 1
Teaching Progressions

Chapter 4 recommended that soccer teachers use the teaching progression: technique practice— skill practice—small-sided game. The teaching progressions for level 1 given in this chapter (and the level 2 and 3 progressions outlined in chapters 6 and 7) list the techniques, drills, skill practices, small-sided games, and soccer fundamentals appropriate for use with players learning the sport.

The materials in chapters 5 and 6 have been arranged according to the recommended teaching progression so that beginning teachers will be able to choose readily the games and drills that will suit the lesson plans they are developing. Chapter 7 discusses functional training, principles of play, and conditioning methods appropriate for older, more advanced soccer players. The level 1 progressions should fit into a soccer unit that includes ten to fifteen practice sessions, and the materials should be easily adapted to fit the needs of beginning students as their skills develop and as their weaknesses become evident.

This chapter begins with the basic techniques of soccer, describing and illustrating fundamentals such as passing and dribbling, and it describes drills useful for technique practice. The basics are followed by specific skill practices and small-sided games.

PASSING TECHNIQUES

In North America, soccer is generally described as a game in which the players kick a ball around a field. Although this is basically true, the description implies a lack of purpose and accurate skill. The soccer teacher should emphasize the difference between just kicking the ball and kicking it accurately. There will always be occasions when players under the pressure of the game give little thought to accuracy, but generally the purpose of kicking the ball should be to pass it to a teammate or to shoot at the goal. That is why practicing passing techniques is fundamental to learning, and teaching, the game of soccer.

Inside of the Foot Pass

The inside of the foot pass should be used when passing accurately over a short distance.

Teaching Points

1. Contact the center of the ball with the flat surface of the inside of the foot (figure 5-1A).
2. Accelerate the lower leg on contact with the ball (figure 5-1B).
3. Follow through after contact with the ball (figure 5-1C).

A   B   C

Figure 5-1

Outside of the Foot Pass

The outside of the foot pass should be used to pass without breaking running stride, to pass to the side, and to curve the path of the ball.

Teaching Points

1. Position yourself at the side of the ball (figure 5-2A).
2. Contact the ball with the outer edge of the foot, toe in (figure 5-2B).
3. Follow through after contact with the ball (figure 5-2C).

A   B   C

Figure 5-2

PASSING PRACTICE

In Pairs

In addition to the drills for pairs listed below, pairs can use the practices outlined for use with a rebound wall (see p. 21).

Drill 1: Through the Tunnel

The two players are positioned 10 yards apart. One player stands with his or her legs wide, and the other player tries to pass the ball through his or her partner's legs (figure 5-3).

Figure 5-3

The inside of the foot pass, the outside of the foot pass, and the instep pass can be used. The passing player makes ten passes at a distance of 10 yards from the other player, first with the right and then with the left foot. The students can record their results on a chart like this one and they can score themselves on the skill check to get valuable feedback on their progress.

Trial	On Target	Missed Target
Right foot		
Left foot		

SKILL CHECK

Points to Look For	Right		Left	
	Yes	No	Yes	No
1. Step forward into the pass				
2. Nonkicking foot beside ball				
3. Contact with inside of foot/outside of foot/instep				
4. Body leaning over the ball				
5. Eyes on the ball				
6. Snap lower leg quickly				
7. Follow through with lower leg				

Drill 2: Circle Drill

One player runs around in a circle while the other passes, using various methods (figure 5-4). The running player makes five passes with each foot (using both the inside and the outside), and then the players change places.

Figure 5-4

Drill 3: In and Out

One player adjusts his or her position by moving in and out in order to vary the power and method used over various distances. Both the inside of the foot pass and the instep pass should be practiced (figure 5-5). Each player repeats the drill ten times with each method.

Figure 5-5

Drill 4: Wall Pass

Player A passes from 5 yards and player B "rebounds" the ball with the inside of the foot for his or her teammate to run on to (figure 5-6). The drill is repeated ten times before the players change places.

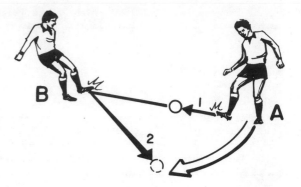

Figure 5-6

Drill 5: Give and Go

Player A passes to player B, who passes back to player A on the move. Player A then gives a wall pass to player B on the move (figure 5-8). The drill repeats until players A and B have each executed ten passes.

Figure 5-7

In Groups of Three or More

Drill 6: Shuttle Run

Player A passes to player B and follows the ball to take player B's place as player B passes to player C (figure 5-7). The drill is repeated, with the three players passing and following the ball, until each of the players has made ten passes without the ball stopping.

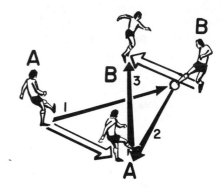

Figure 5-8

Drill 7: Square Passing

The players pass and move to a new position within a 10-yard square (figure 5-9). The drill repeats until each of the players has executed ten passes without stopping the ball and while keeping it within the prescribed area.

Figure 5-9

RECEIVING AND BALL CONTROL TECHNIQUES

Juggling

Receiving techniques should be practiced individually before being used in realistic drills. For this reason, juggling (or ball familiarity) activities are valuable preliminaries. They help the players judge the weight and feel of the ball on different parts of their bodies. The use of set practices is advised. However, it is important that players perform the practices exactly as they are specified so that the players can become accustomed to reacting to the movement of the ball. (See the instructions on juggling practice given in evaluation chart 8-2, p.159.)

Although valuable for improving the players' sensitivity and balance, juggling is only a means to an end and not an end in itself. A player's ability to bring the ball down is more important than his or her ability to keep it up indefinitely.

The techniques used for receiving a ball or bringing it under control vary according to the flight or direction the ball is taking. Receiving involves *movement;* the player should move to a position in the ball's line of flight or in the direction the ball is heading in order to be prepared to receive it. *Decision* is also an important factor in receiving; the player should decide early which method should be used, but he or she should be flexible enough to react to a ball that changes direction. *Preparation* is also vital; the player should be in a balanced position ready to present the controlling surface in order to be prepared to receive a ball. And *relaxation* should be emphasized; the player should relax the controlling surface of his or her body by cushioning or giving with the ball to bring it under control and then move away easily.

Moving to the Direction of the Ball

It is important for the player to get into position behind the flight of the ball in order to be ready to receive it.

Teaching Points

1. Be quick off the mark in order to meet the ball (figure 5-10A).
2. Get ready to receive the ball (figure 5-10B).
3. Put some part of your body behind the ball so that you can stop its progress (figure 5-10C).

A   B   C

Figure 5-10

Wedging the Ball on the Ground

The ball can be wedged against the ground to bring the ball under control with the sole of the foot (figure 5-11), the inside of the foot (figure 5-12), or the outside of the foot (figure 5-13).

Teaching Points

1. Judge where the ball is going to drop (figures 5-11A, 5-12A, 5-13A).
2. Contact the ball between the foot and the ground as the ball contacts the ground (figures 5-11B, 5-12B, 5-13B).
3. Sweep the ball away under control (figures 5-11C, 5-12C, 5-13C).

A   B   C

Figure 5-11

A   B   C

Figure 5-12

A   B   C

Figure 5-13

RECEIVING AND BALL CONTROL PRACTICE

By Individuals

Wedging should be practiced individually until the students can control the ball with each foot on each of six attempts.

Drill 1

The player practices wedging methods by dropping the ball and timing the contact of the foot on the ball as the ball touches the ground. Each method of wedging should be used three times for each foot. And after the player has stopped the ball each time, he or she should move off quickly with the ball under control.

Drill 2

The player throws the ball up just above the height of his head and then wedges the ball with the sole, inside, or outside of the foot on the first bounce of the ball, after which the player moves off quickly with the ball under control.

Drill 3

Players who have learned to juggle the ball can do this drill. The player juggles the ball and then plays it high in the air and finally brings it down under control by using each of the wedging techniques.

In Pairs

These pair drills can also be practiced by individual players using a rebound wall.

Drill 4: Pass and Control

Two players positioned 10 yards apart pass and control the ball with the insides of their feet (figure 5-14).

Figure 5-14

Drill 5: Control and Turn

Two players control the ball with the out-sides of their feet and turn in the same motion before they stop to return the ball to their partner (figure 5-15).

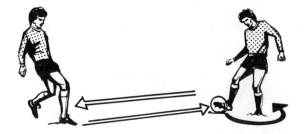

Figure 5-15

Drill 6: Throw-in

One player throws the ball in to the other from 10 yards away. The receiving player wedges the ball as it bounces with the inside, outside, and sole of the foot (figure 5-16).

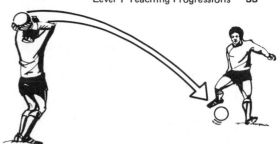

Figure 5-16

TECHNIQUES FOR RUNNING WITH THE BALL

After the students have learned how to control the ball, they are ready to begin practicing the techniques for dribbling, or running with, the ball. Initially, the players should be allowed to run with the ball in order to familiarize themselves with the basic techniques: (1) running with the ball close to the feet and contacting the ball with the outsides and insides of their feet; (2) running with the ball at various paces, stopping, sprinting, jogging, etc.; (3) weaving in and out while using the insides and outsides of their feet to control the ball; (4) swerving with or without playing the ball; and (5) twisting and turning with the ball in a confined space. Then they should practice more refined techniques for running with the ball.

Running in Close Control

Close control is essential for keeping possession of the ball in situations when the player is being closely marked.

Teaching Points

1. Take short strides when running with the ball (figure 5-17A).
2. Play the ball as often as possible with the insides, outsides, and soles of your feet (figure 5-17B).
3. Look down to watch the ball when defenders are ready to tackle you (figure 5-17C).

A   B   C

Figure 5-17

Running in Space

Players should learn to cover distance quickly when they are running with the ball in an open space.

Teaching Points

1. Take full running strides (figure 5-18A).
2. Play the ball with the outside of the foot on every full stride but don't kick it too far ahead of you (figure 5-18B).
3. Look up to see the space around you and to watch for passing possibilities (figure 5-18C).

Figure 5-18

RUNNING WITH THE BALL PRACTICE

By Individuals

Drill 1: Dodge and Weave

Inside a 10-yard square grid or a confined area, the players move about, feinting, dodging, and swerving to avoid bumping into other players or contacting other balls (figure 5-19).

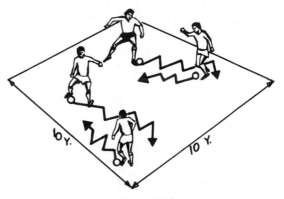

Figure 5-19

Drill 2: Circle Drill

The player runs with the ball around the center circle of the gym or field, changing direction on command. First, the player uses the inside of a foot while running with the ball in a free stride. Then, he or she changes direction by stopping the ball with the sole of a foot and rolling the ball back in the opposite direction without losing sight of it (figure 5-20).

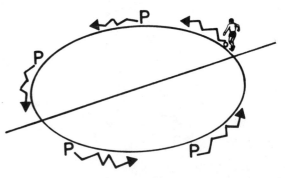

Figure 5-20

Drill 3: Give and Go

The player runs with the ball as in the circle drill. But he or she is looking up for a signal from a teammate or the coach, who is in the center of the circle pointing, not calling, for the ball (figure 5-21). This encourages the player to keep his or her head up. Then, when the signal is given by the person in the center of the circle, the player makes a push pass to the center person and runs forward to receive the return pass and continue running with the ball.

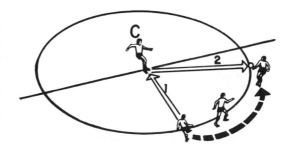

Figure 5-21

Drill 4: Circle Sprint

As in give and go, the player runs around the circle until he or she sees a signal. Then, the player sprints across the circle with the ball and continues traveling around the circle (figure 5-22). The player should keep his or her head up and drive into the open space when the signal is given.

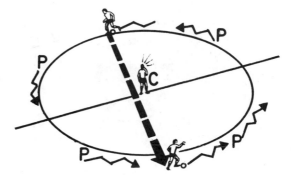

Figure 5-22

Drill 5: Slalom

Again, the player runs around the circle with the ball until signaled to weave in and out of the other players in the circle for one round and then return to the circle (figure 5-23).

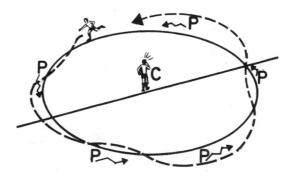

Figure 5-23

TACKLING TECHNIQUE

Front Block

The front block is used to challenge an opponent for possession of the ball when two players meet face to face.

Teaching Points

1. Keep your eyes on the ball (figure 5-24A).
2. Watch your timing; contact the ball with the inside of your foot just as your opponent touches the ball (figure 5-24B).
3. Step into the tackle, carrying your weight through the center of the ball and supporting yourself with the other leg, which is behind and to the side of the ball; keep your knees bent (figure 5-24C).
4. After making block contact, follow through by rolling the ball over your opponent's foot (figure 5-25A).
5. Or, after making block contact, follow through by forcing the ball through your opponent's legs and receive it on his or her other side (figure 5-25B).

A   B   C

Figure 5-24

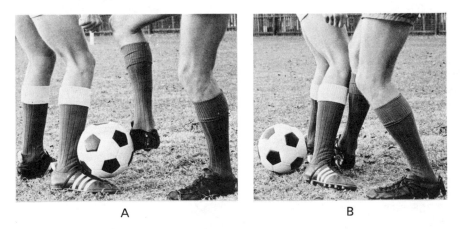

A   B

Figure 5-25

TACKLING PRACTICE

In Pairs

Drill 1

Methods for winning the ball after contact with an opponent in possession of the ball can be practiced by having the players assume the contact position they would use in a front block tackle. When the coach signals, they attempt to win the ball by pushing it through the opponents' legs or rolling it over their feet. Then they run with the ball to the end of the line before being tackled again (figure 5-26).

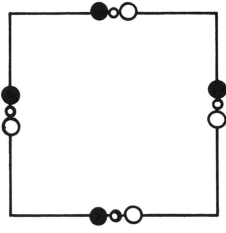

Figure 5-26

With Seventeen Players

Drill 2: Dribbling and Tackling

The drill is played in four square coaching grids or boxes marked on the floor or field. Seventeen players are involved in play in the four boxes (figure 5-27).

Figure 5-27

Rules

1. One player faces another player in each box. There are players positioned in the corners of the boxes. One player in the box tries to dribble the ball to a corner while the other player in the box tries to take the ball. When a player with a ball reaches a corner, the corner player takes the ball back into play and the other player takes the corner position and rests.
2. The player with the ball may not return to the same corner he or she has just left.
3. The tackler must move to the center of the square on a changeover to give the new player a fair start.
4. A ball that is kicked out of play should be returned to the square by the nonoffending player.

KICKING AND SHOOTING TECHNIQUE

Instep Drive

The instep drive is used to pass the ball over long distances and to shoot at the goal.

Teaching Points

1. Step up to the ball (figure 5-28A).
2. Contact the ball with your instep (on the laces of your shoe) with your toe down and your knee bent over the ball (figure 5-28B).
3. Snap the lower leg quickly.
4. Follow through after the ball (figure 5-28C).

A   B   C

Figure 5-28

KICKING AND SHOOTING PRACTICE

In Pairs

Drill 1

Between two markers placed 2 yards apart, one player passes the ball to a teammate from 10 yards away. The pass is made with an inside, outside, or instep drive (figure 5-29).

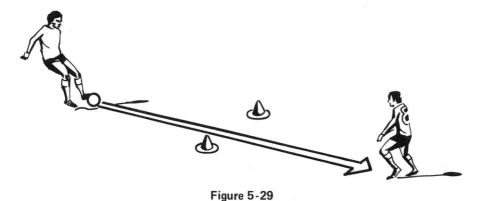

Figure 5-29

In Threes

Drill 2: Score

A goalkeeper stationed between two markers tries to stop shots at the goal from two other players, who shoot with an instep drive alternately from opposite sides of the goal (figure 5-30). The goalkeeper rolls the ball out for the player to make the shot. After the goalkeeper stops one player's shot, he or she turns around and rolls the ball to the other player, who then takes a shot.

Figure 5-30

Drill 3: Pass and Shoot

The two shooting players start out 20 yards apart at the halfway line. They run toward the goal, passing the ball back and forth between them. When they reach the penalty area line, the player with the ball makes a shot (figure 5-31). They continue playing until each player has made ten shots with the instep of each foot. The players should exchange places and continue practicing until all three are able to score consistently.

Figure 5-31

Drill 4: Give and Go

One player outside the penalty area passes to another inside. The second player passes the ball back to the first player, who then makes a shot (figure 5-32). Each player should take ten shots with each foot. All the players should practice until they are able to score consistently.

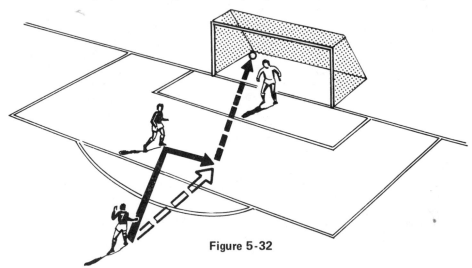

Figure 5-32

GOALKEEPING TECHNIQUES

Handling the Ball

A low ball can be handled by bending closer to the ball down on one knee (figure 5-33) or bending with straight legs (figure 5-34).

Teaching Points

1. Get behind the line of the ball (figure 5-33A).
2. Get down on one knee and place your body behind the ball; have your hands ready (figure 5-33B).
3. Collect the ball into the pit of your stomach and move quickly away with the ball (figure 5-33C).
4. Or, get behind the line of the ball and stand with knees straight (figure 5-34A).
5. Bend from the hips with your legs together (figure 5-34B).
6. Collect the ball with your outstretched hands (figure 5-34C).

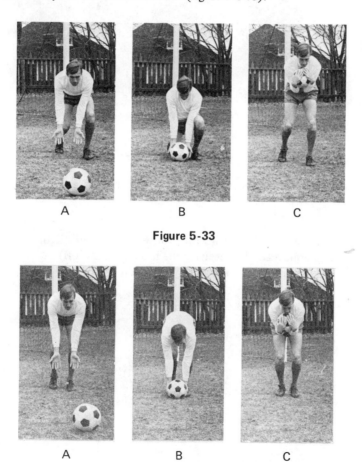

Figure 5-33

Figure 5-34

Falling on the Ball

The player should use the hands to stop a shot when there isn't enough time to get his or her whole body behind the ball.

Teaching Points

1. Fold on your legs and trunk to get down behind the ball (figure 5-35A).
2. Lead with your hands and arms to stop the ball (figure 5-35A).
3. Use your whole body as a block behind your hands and arms (figure 5-35B).
4. After you've collected the ball, protect it by rolling over and folding tight around the ball (figure 5-35C).

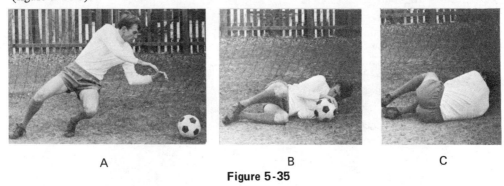

A   B   C

Figure 5-35

Catching the Ball Waist High

This technique can be used for safely collecting a ball shot at waist level.

Teaching Points

1. Take a balanced position behind the ball with your weight forward (figure 5-36A).
2. Keep your hands and arms ready for receiving the ball (figure 5-36B).
3. Collect the ball and give with your body on impact (figure 5-36C).

A   B   C

Figure 5-36

Catching the Ball Chest or Head High

This technique is best used for balls that come toward the goal at the level of the goalkeeper's chest or head.

Teaching Points

1. Meet the ball as early as possible (figure 5-37A).
2. Keep your hands raised toward the ball, with your fingers spread wide behind the ball (figure 5-37B).
3. Contact the ball in front of your head, give on contact with it, and bring it down to your chest (figure 5-37C).

A   B   C

Figure 5-37

GOALKEEPING PRACTICE

In Pairs

Drill 1: Pickup Drill

One player stands between two markers establishing a goal line. That player rolls the ball out to the second player, who shoots the ball straight back with an instep drive (figure 5-38). The goalkeeping player then picks up the ball and returns it to the other player. As the players gain skill picking up the ball, they can change the drill by having the passing player shoot to the left or right of the goalkeeper so that he or she has to move behind the ball before picking it up.

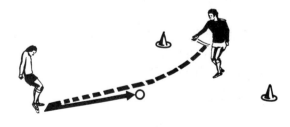

Figure 5-38

In Threes

Drill 2: Stop and Throw

A goalkeeper stands between two markers or flags with a player 20 yards away on each side of the goal. The goalkeeper throws the ball to the feet of one of the players (a javelin throw), and he or she brings the ball under control and shoots with an instep drive (figure 5-39). The goalkeeper then stops the ball, turns, and throws it to the other player.

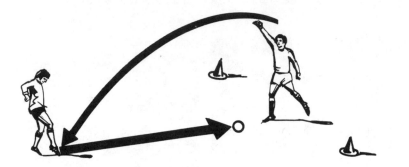

Figure 5-39

HEADING TECHNIQUES

Heading probably causes beginning soccer players more apprehension than any other part of the game. The players' initial fear of being hit on the head is understandable, particularly when the ball is heavy or wet. Some children who are quite confident in attacking the ball may experience pain when they make a poor contact with the ball, and this may dampen their enthusiasm. Therefore, coaches and teachers should recognize the problems they may have with beginners or with players who have poor technique. Practice in the basic heading techniques before the players are faced with a game situation is always advisable.

Face-on Heading

The face-on heading technique is useful for heading the ball powerfully toward the goal and for clearing the ball from defensive players.

Teaching Points

1. Start from a balanced position facing the oncoming ball (figure 5-40A).
2. Use your legs to propel your trunk and head forward to meet the ball.
3. Contact the ball flat on your forehead above your eyes (figure 5-40B).
4. Follow through after contact with the ball by directing the ball with a powerful extension of your neck (figure 5-40C).

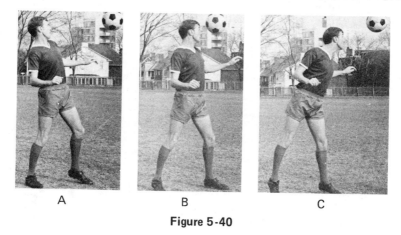

Figure 5-40

Heading to the Side

This heading technique is used to direct the ball to a teammate or to score a goal.

Teaching Point

Turn your head and neck on contact with the ball to change the direction of its flight (figure 5-41).

Figure 5-41

HEADING PRACTICE

In Pairs

Drill 1: Headers

Two players use a coaching grid or two goals set up 10 yards apart to practice scoring goals with headers (figure 5-42). One teammate throws the ball underhanded to his or her teammate, who tries to head the ball back through the goal. Each player should attempt six headers, and the partners should keep score.

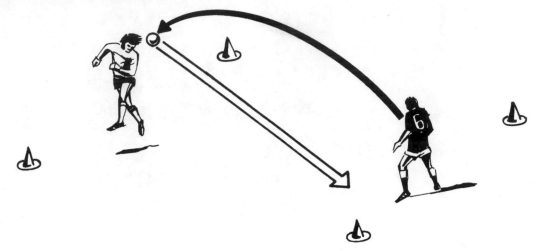

Figure 5-42

Drill 2: Head to Toe

Two players practice passing the ball by heading (figure 5-43). Player A throws the ball to player B, who heads the ball down to the ground for player A to control. The drill is repeated until each player has successfully headed a pass six times.

Figure 5-43

In Threes

Drill 3: Head to Side

Player A throws the ball to player B, who deflects the ball to the side for player C to control and run with. Player C then throws to player A, who heads the ball to player B, and so on until each player has headed successfully six times (figure 5-44).

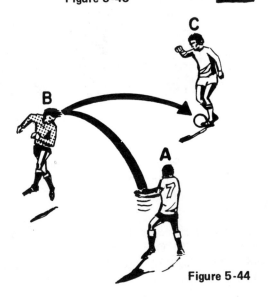

Figure 5-44

Drill 4: Score

Player A serves to player B, who attempts to head the ball past player C, who is acting as the goalkeeper (figure 5-45). Each player takes six headers, and the team keeps score. The players should be coached to direct the ball down off the ground in order to confuse the goalkeeper.

Figure 5-45

Drill 5: Diving Header

One player throws the ball to another player, who attempts a diving header while kneeling on the ground (figure 5-46). The diving header can be practiced from a position on all fours, also. The player stretches forward to head the ball before landing in a push-up position.

Figure 5-46

PASSING AND SHOOTING SKILL PRACTICE

Passing and shooting are best taught in "live" situations. The practices described in this section are designed for use in confined areas (boxes or grids marked out with corner flags, extra balls, or other equipment) on or off the playing field. The dimensions of the playing areas can be varied to suit the students' level of ability. Squares with sides between 10 and 20 yards long are appropriate for beginners. These competitive practices can put three players against one, four versus two, three versus two, two against one, three against three, three versus four, five against five, and seven versus seven. The objective is to be in possession of the ball and the emphasis is on constant movement (see figure 5-47).

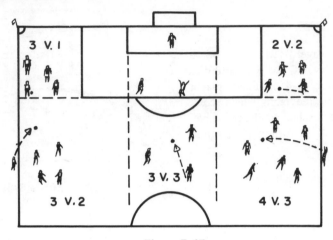

Figure 5-47

Basic Passing Practice

This is a fairly easy practice in which the players can develop a feel for the different kinds of contact. The players should try to keep possession of the ball and they should aim for a specific number of successful passes without interception—for example, three or six apiece (figure 5-48).

Coaching Points

1. The teacher should stress that the players should run off the ball to give the player on the ball more alternatives.
2. The players will naturally assume a triangular formation in which little movement is necessary to receive the ball (figure 5-48A). They will have to be taught how to move intelligently to give support to the player with the ball. For example, the player at point 1 has less space and time than he or she would have at point 2 but has a better receiving angle at point 1 (figure 5-48B).

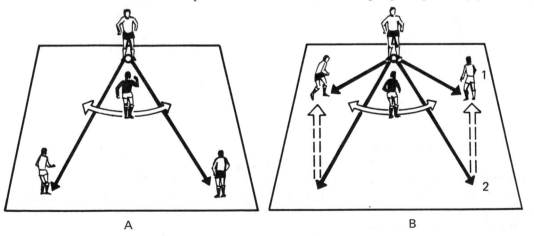

A   B

Figure 5-48

Pass and Move (or Give and Go)

One player makes the pass and then follows the ball to give support to the receiving player (figure 5-49).

Coaching Point

The player on the ball can be told to point where he or she wants his or her teammate to take up position.

Figure 5-49

Blind Side Running and Cutting

The player with the ball passes and then cuts across the defender's path without obstructing him or her while the other teammate runs on the defender's blind side to create a new passing alternative (figure 5-50).

Figure 5-50

Square Passing

In this practice, the target is either a corner or one side of the playing square. The defender tends to leave the ball carrier and cover more space, and the offensive team is forced to find ways of getting past the defender without lying behind him or her (going offside).

The receiver (player A) draws the defender toward him or her or moves in front to collect the ball, and then player A sends a square pass to player B. If the defender moves across to intercept the ball, then player B sends a square pass back to player A. If the feeder (player C) follows the pass, then he or she can create another alternative square pass on player A's left side (figure 5-51).

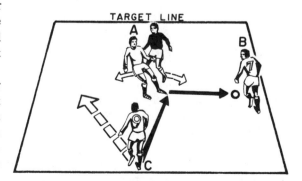

Figure 5-51

GOALKEEPING SKILL PRACTICE

Goalie in the Middle

Two players pass the ball back and forth in order to keep possession while a goalkeeper attempts to intercept the ball by diving (figure 5-52). When the goalkeeper is successful, he or she rolls the ball back to the passing players. Practice should be done for a minute, and then the players should rest before repeating the practice two more times.

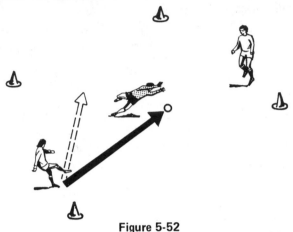

Figure 5-52

Courage

The goalkeeper defends a makeshift goal against a player running with the ball who is trying to dribble the ball over the goal line (figure 5-53). At the same time he or she is defending the goal, the goalkeeper is trying to intercept the ball. The players should practice for one minute, rest, and then repeat the practice three more times.

DRIBBLING SKILL PRACTICE

Dribbling techniques can be practiced around the grid, with the defender restricted to one side of the line and the dribbler the other. The target for the ball carrier is reaching one end of the line (figure 5-54). The defender should anticipate the movements of the ball carrier and stay beside the carrier. In subsequent practices, the defender can be allowed to strike for the ball when it touches the line.

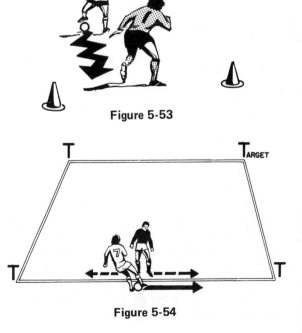

Figure 5-53

Figure 5-54

TACKLING SKILL PRACTICE

A more realistic skill practice for both dribbling and tackling is this one-on-one situation inside a grid. The target is to reach any side except the one behind the ball carrier (figure 5-55). When the ball carrier succeeds in reaching the target, a supporting player takes over the ball.

Figure 5-55

SHOOTING SKILL PRACTICE

The shooting skill practice begins with the first shooter in line making a shot from a cut back while he or she is being chased by an opponent (take turn about). The ball should be played in softly so that the attacker can come off his or her opponent and meet the ball early and on the move (figure 5-56).

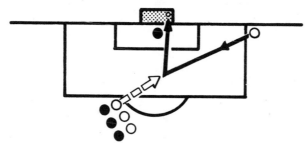

Figure 5-56

Then, the players should work on building up to closer cover by opposing players, with the receivers moving to meet the ball (figure 5-57).

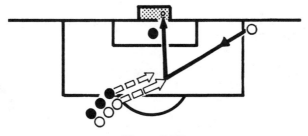

Figure 5-57

Next, an alternative should be introduced into the play. When the receiver is not in a position to shoot, he or she should pass the ball to a supporting player, who then makes the shot (figure 5-58).

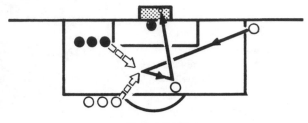

Figure 5-58

Gradually, the practice can be built up into a functional practice in which the players are covered as they work on alternatives for getting a shot away (figure 5-59).

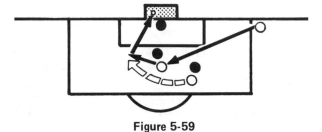

Figure 5-59

The practice can be done as a two versus one competition in the area of the penalty box, with two players interpassing and shooting against one defender (figure 5-60).

Figure 5-60

RECEIVING SKILL PRACTICE

Two versus One

The server throws the ball from the far corner of a square playing area. The receiver controls the ball and passes it to his or her teammate before the server is able to intercept or tackle (figure 5-61). In the same situation, practice can be done with receiving by thigh, chest, and head.

Figure 5-61

Less Time and Space

In a three versus one situation, the server (player S) throws the ball from the center of the grid. The receiving player has to react quickly in order to control the ball (figure 5-62). The use of wedge passing and screening are necessary skills.

Figure 5-62

Two versus Two Receiving Game

The players work in pairs. The server throws the ball to his or her teammate, who is allowed one touch on the ball to bring it under control. screening the ball from the opponent before picking up the ball to return it to the server (figure 5-63). When the ball is not controlled cleanly, the opponent may challenge and try to intercept the ball. If he or she takes possession of the ball, the game continues with the player and his or her teammate throwing and receiving the ball until it is again intercepted.

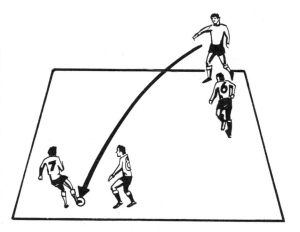

Figure 5-63

HEADING SKILL PRACTICE

Once they have overcome their initial fear of contacting the ball with their heads, the players may develop a secondary fear—contact with other players. Many players master heading techniques and then find that they are afraid to use them in a game because they don't want to risk running into an opponent while heading the ball. In this situation, the coach again should work to build up the confidence of apprehensive players by gradually exposing them to more realistic game situations. He or she should help the players recognize which techniques are best used under pressure. The grid system of practice is very useful for coaching heading. As in other skill-learning situations, the coach can control the distance between opposing players and, by limiting the space available, control the amount of time the players have to execute techniques as well.

Defensive Heading

The ball is introduced into the playing area by a high service from a player, who immediately becomes a challenger. The receiver heads the ball to a supporting player (figure 5-64).

Figure 5-64

Then, the players practice in the same situation but with less space and time (figure 5-65). The practice develops the players' ability to assess their options quickly and head the ball down powerfully.

Figure 5-65

In another practice situation, the receiver takes a long service from the far corner of the gird and with closer opposition (figure 5-66). The players should practice heading down for power back to the server or down to support. They should also practice jumping with one and both feet.

Figure 5-66

Offensive Heading

Attacking involves the same principles as defending and clearing and should be approached in the same way. In fact, it is often useful for the coach to teach both offensive and defensive strategies for the same situation. He or she should show both the defensive and offensive players exactly why they succeeded in one instance and what they should do to improve their chances of winning. Much of the attacking team's success in the heading practice depends on the service of the receiver.

In the situation illustrated in figure 5-67, the offense can take the advantage. If the serve is a low ball played at head height, the receiver can cushion the ball and head it down to a supporting player. Here the attacker is involved in a typical playing environment and is shown an acceptable solution. As a consequence, the opponent marks tighter, but this shouldn't cause the attacker further problems.

Figure 5-67

When the service is high, it becomes difficult for the receiver to play the ball back, so the attacker has to deflect the ball past the defender to advancing support (figure 5-68). Good judgment on timing and takeoff is vital to the attackers' game as well as to the defenders'.

Figure 5-68

The attackers can begin using power heading and diving heading in the situation illustrated in figure 5-69. These heading techniques give the players sufficient space and time to move, and, once their confidence has increased, the space in the practice grid can be closed up.

Figure 5-69

SMALL-SIDED GAMES

Four versus Two

The object of this game, besides keeping possession of the ball, is getting the ball between the defenders by trying to catch them lying square (in line) (figure 5-70).

Figure 5-70

Three versus Three

The players use the goal and the center circle as targets for attacking and defending and the width of the penalty box as the field area (figure 5-71).

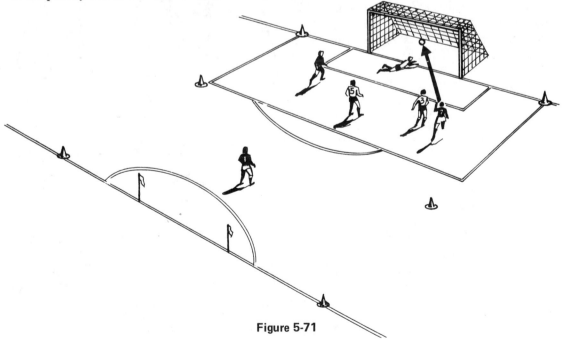

Figure 5-71

Mini Soccer

Mini soccer is useful for practicing skills in a game situation in which there is more opportunity for touching the ball and all the players have a good chance of showing improvement. The diagram of the field (figure 5-72) illustrates a field size recommended for players between six and eight years old.

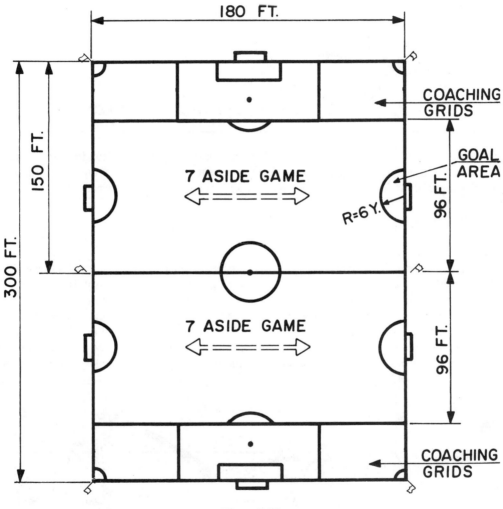

Figure 5-72

6

Level 2 Teaching Progressions

The skills and techniques introduced on this level should build upon the foundation of basic skills laid in level 1. However, the teacher should feel free to use the progressions from levels 1 and 3 when alternative methods are needed to help the players achieve an objective or advance their skill.

WARMUP GAMES

Heading Game

Heading games can be difficult to construct outside of regular soccer play because services for heading are irregular and it can be difficult to keep the game going continuously. However, this game in which the players advance with the ball, throw it up and head it toward the goal to score, or catch it is a good warmup. When the sequence breaks down and the ball goes out of play, the opposing team can restart the game with a throw-in. The game can be varied by having the players head the ball continuously and restart with a header, or the ball can be passed between the players like a basketball and the heading shot can be set up at the goal. The defense would attempt to intercept the ball with their heads.

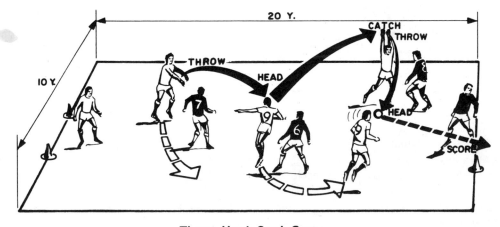

Throw, Head, Catch Game

58

Passing Games

The best warmup of all is probably some variation of regular soccer, for example, indoor soccer or five aside soccer, depending on the facilities available. Played as an open running game with some conditions set (for example, two-touch passing or first-time passing), the games allow enough movement for adequate warmup and become good coaching vehicles.

The games can be varied by using spare players on the attacking side who change sides when the ball does. This is invaluable practice for young players learning the principles of soccer play, both offensive and defensive.

Rotation Game

The players are numbered from 1 to 5 or 7. The ball is advanced from player 1 to player 2 and so on. If the ball is intercepted by number 3 of the opposition, he or she continues the rotation to player 4 of his or her own team. The game demands intelligent running and positioning and distributes the workload evenly.

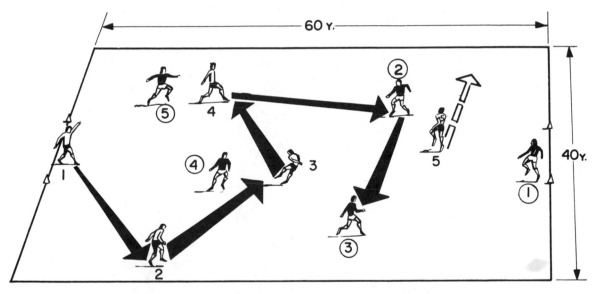

Rotation Game

Numbers Game

The players are numbered from 1 to 5. This game is best played indoors with two teams of five, each team defending an end wall of a gymnasium. When the coach calls out numbers, the players called from each team play against each other to try to score past the defending wall of players. The game involves all of the players equally and provides good coaching situations. Players can be called out singly or in groups (two versus two or three versus three) to bring out a passing dimension to the practice.

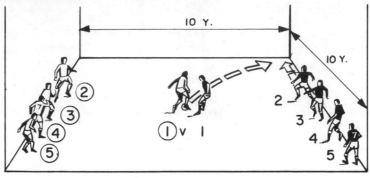

Numbers Game

Four Goals

There are four goals, each defended by a pair of players; two pairs play together against two other pairs and attack either of their two goals. Again, this game is useful for coaching principles and responsibilities.

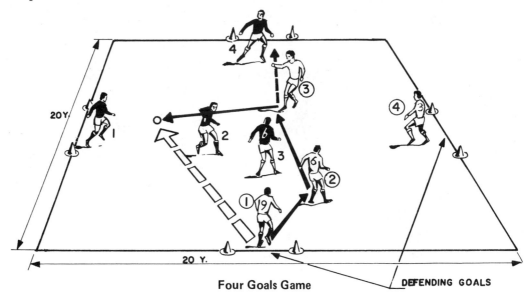

Four Goals Game   **DEFENDING GOALS**

Grid Games

The grid system, or any small playing area, lends itself to a variety of passing games, including three versus one in one area and four versus three across two grids. Expanding the playing area and using more players produce more player involvement and coaching situations. Also, when the grid games are done as a part of pressure training, they become extremely demanding and result in increased conditioning. The coach should know how to use specific practices to produce the intended effect.

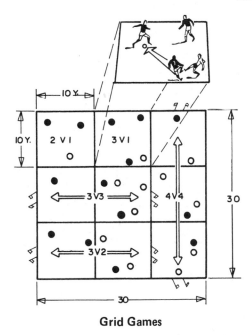

Grid Games

Dribbling Game

In a grid or in a small-sided area, the players must keep possession of the ball (no passing is allowed) and dribble it over an end line. In one variation that produces more involvement, the players must beat one other player before they are allowed to pass the ball. The coach can control the conditions in the game in order to accentuate running with the ball.

Tackling Game

The coach can also control this game to emphasize tackling or interception; however, when the players move the ball around, it is difficult to focus on tackling. So, after tackling skills have been taught in other situations, a dribbling condition should be integrated into this practice in order to increase the players' opportunities to tackle.

TECHNIQUES FOR LIFTING THE BALL

The techniques of chipping and lifting the ball can be learned by having the players adjust their body positions and areas of contact with the ball. The players find it easier to lift the ball when it is rolling toward them, and they can achieve the sensation of getting the contact foot under the ball as it rolls up, instead of having to attempt to kick a stationary ball.

Lifted Pass/Shot

This technique is used to lift the ball over a defender and pass, to shoot high at the goal, and to take corner kicks.

Teaching Points

1. Approach the ball at an angle.
2. Make a long last stride toward the ball.
3. Place your supporting foot to the side and behind the ball.
4. Make a long, free-leg swing and straighten your leg when your foot contacts the ball (figure 6-1A).
5. Contact the ball with the inside of your instep and with a firm ankle (figure 6-2B).
6. Lean back and lift the ball (figure 6-1C).

A   B   C

Figure 6-1

Chip Pass/Shot

This technique is used for lifting the ball sharply over opposing players to pass or shoot.

Teaching Points

1. Stand directly behind the point toward which the ball is rolling.
2. Bend your lower leg only when the ball approaches you.
3. Stab your lower leg at the ball with your foot held firm (figure 6-2A).
4. Feel the ball rolling up on your instep as you jab your foot under the ball (figure 6-2B).
5. Don't follow through with a leg swing and the ball will rise sharply (figure 6-2C).

A   B   C

Figure 6-2

PRACTICE LIFTING THE BALL

In Pairs

Drill 1: Chip, Control, Pass

Two players practice lifting and chipping the ball by playing the ball the first time (without control) to pass it to the teammate, who controls the ball and rolls it back (figure 6-3). Each player takes six turns with each foot.

Figure 6-3

In Threes

Drill 2: Over the Top

A goalkeeper is positioned between two cones for a makeshift goal, with a player on either side of him or her. The players practice lifting the ball over or past the goalkeeper (figure 6-4). The goalkeeper starts the drill by rolling the ball out to one of the players. The player chips the ball over the top to the player on the other side of the goal; the other player controls the ball and rolls it back to the goalkeeper, who starts the drill over again. The players can use an actual goal to practice keeping the ball under the crossbar.

Figure 6-4

TECHNIQUES FOR STRIKING THE BOUNCING BALL

Unfortunately, the ball doesn't always stay on the ground for the players to kick, so they often have to pass or shoot a bouncing ball before an opponent can get in the way.

Half Volley

This pass is used for shooting or for clearance kicking.

Teaching Points

1. Judge the bounce of the ball and step in to contact it as it touches the ground (figure 6-5A).
2. Make contact with your instep or the inside of your foot and with your knee bent over the ball (figure 6-5B).
3. Swing your leg and follow through as the ball touches the ground (figure 6-5C).

A   B   C

Figure 6-5

Side Volley

The side volley is used for shooting powerfully and for clearing the ball from the defense.

Teaching Points

1. Judge the flight of the ball.
2. Adopt a balanced position (figure 6-6A).
3. Contact the ball with your instep (laces), toe down (figure 6-6B).
4. Follow through in the direction of the ball (figure 6-6C).

A   B   C

Figure 6-6

VOLLEYING PRACTICE

By Individuals

Drill 1: Drop Kick

The player practices the half and side volleys by dropping the ball from his or her hands, letting it bounce once, and then timing contact with the ball and rebounding the ball from a wall or passing it to a teammate.

Drill 2: Rebound

The player starts the drill by throwing the ball against a rebound wall and letting it bounce once before driving it back to the wall with a side or a half volley (figure 6-7). The player should try to rebound the ball continuously by kicking it when it rebounds from the wall.

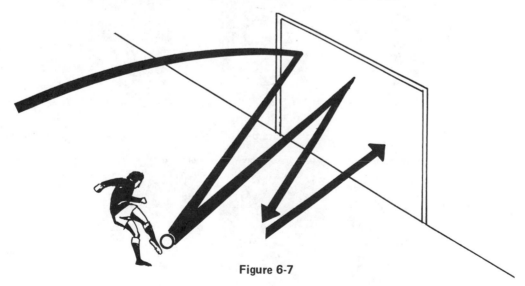

Figure 6-7

RECEIVING TECHNIQUES

Controlling the Ball in the Air

The ball can be controlled in the air before an opponent can intercept it by meeting it with the instep, the thigh, or the chest.

Teaching Points

1. Judge the drop of the ball (figures 6-8A, 6-9A, 6-10A, and 6-11A).
2. Relax the controlling surface of your body (figures 6-8B, 6-9B, 6-10B, and 6-11B).
3. Move off with the ball under control (figures 6-8C, 6-9C, 6-10C, and 6-11C).

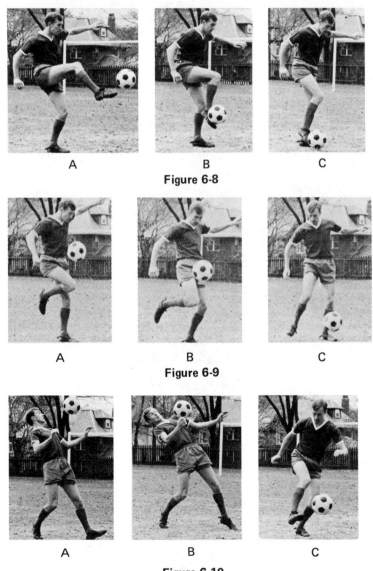

A   B   C

Figure 6-8

A   B   C

Figure 6-9

A   B   C

Figure 6-10

A   B   C

Figure 6-11

RECEIVING PRACTICE

By Individuals

Drill 1: Drop Kick

The player receives the ball in the air by kicking the ball from his or her hands and then timing contact with the ball as it bounces.

Drill 2: Rebound

The player throws the ball against the rebound wall or has a teammate pass it to him or her, and then the player controls the ball and passes it back toward the wall or the teammate (figure 6-12).

Figure 6-12

DRIBBLING TECHNIQUES

Dribbling is best taught in live situations hand in hand with tackling and interception since both skills are played in direct opposition and attackers and defenders can be coached in the same situation. The conventional methods of dribbling and tackling are described in the following pages.

Inside and Outside of the Foot Dribbling

This method of dribbling is used to change direction and to avoid an opponent.

Teaching Points

1. Play the ball in a definite direction with the inside of your foot (figure 6-13A).
2. Quickly step over the ball (figure 6-13B).
3. Change direction and pace by moving away quickly and playing the ball with the outside of your foot (figure 6-13C).

| A | B | C |

Figure 6-13

Screening

This type of dribbling should be used to shield the ball from the opponent and prevent him or her from tackling.

Teaching Points

1. Keep your body between the ball and your opponent without leaning on him or her (obstruction) (figure 6-14A).
2. Be aware of both the ball and your opponent.
3. Quickly alter your position when your opponent moves (figure 6-14B).
4. Use controlling techniques: tap the ball with the inside and outside of your foot, roll the ball forward and pull it back with the sole of your foot, holding it at a distance with the sole of your foot (figure 6-14C).

Figure 6-14

TACKLING TECHNIQUES

Side Block

The side block is used to challenge an opponent from the side or the rear.

Teaching Points

1. Approach the player with the ball from the side (figure 6-15A).
2. Step in close to the ball, supporting foot level with the ball (figure 6-15B).
3. Pivot quickly on your foot to contact the ball in the front block position (figure 6-15B).

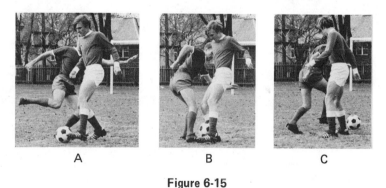

Figure 6-15

Heel Tackle

The heel tackle is used to challenge an opponent moving at speed.

Teaching Points

1. Approach from the rear, keeping your eyes on the ball (figure 6-16A).
2. Lift the leg nearest the ball over it, blocking it with your heel (figure 6-16B).
3. Follow through to recover the ball, turning to control the ball (figure 6-16C).

Figure 6-16

Slide Block

The slide block tackle is used to take the ball away from the opponent from the rear.

Teaching Points

1. Approach from the rear as close as possible to the player with the ball (figure 6-17A).
2. Fold your inside leg and go down on your side, breaking your fall with your hand and arm (figure 6-17B).
3. Swing your inside leg around and contact the ball with your instep in a block position (figure 6-17C).

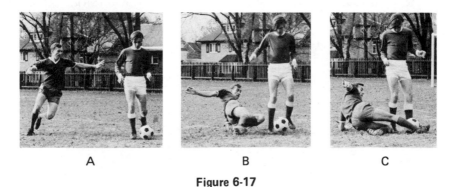

Figure 6-17

DRIBBLING AND TACKLING PRACTICE

Four-Person Drill

The player with the ball under control runs against an opponent, who is restricted to a position on a line between two grids. The player with the ball changes pace, swerves, feints, and screens in order to avoid the defender and reach the target line (T) (figure 6-18). After the player has scored, a supporting player repeats the drill.

Coaching Points

1. The attacking player should commit the defender by running quickly at him or her and should force the defender back on his or her heels.
2. The attacker should commit the defender to one direction rather than running straight at him or her.
3. The attacker should change pace and direction so that the defender has to check and chase.

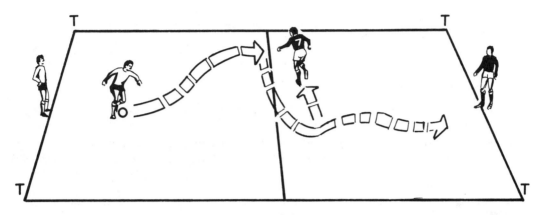

Figure 6-18

GOALKEEPING TECHNIQUES

Handling a ball that is "crossed" or played high into the goal area from the side of the field causes problems for goalkeepers when they don't come off their goal line and outjump their opponents who are trying to head the ball into the goal.

Cutting Out "Crosses"

This technique is used to pick the ball out of the air before it bounces into the danger area.

Teaching Points

1. Take a long last stride before your one-foot takeoff (figure 6-19A).
2. Take the ball as high as possible in front of your head (figure 6-19B).
3. Keep your knee up for protection.
4. Land on both feet and crouch down to protect the ball (figure 6-19C).

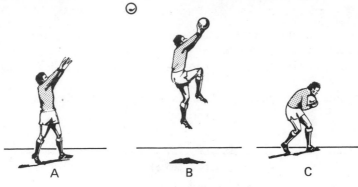

Figure 6-19

Narrowing the Shooting Angle

Goalkeeper A, by staying on the goal line, is leaving much more of the goal open than is goalkeeper B, who has narrowed the angle of the shot by coming off the line, thus leaving a much smaller area of the goal vulnerable (figure 6-20). However, the goalkeeper should not go too far off the line because this would make it easy for an attacker to chip the ball over his or her head and into the goal.

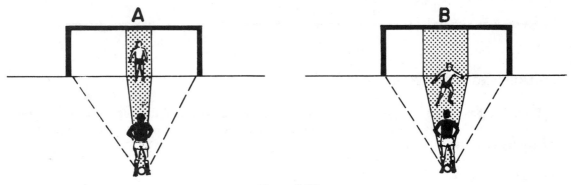

Figure 6-20

Throwing the Ball—Javelin Style

The goalkeeper uses this technique to throw the ball to a teammate over a short distance.

Teaching Points

1. Take the ball in two hands and look for a receiver.
2. Take the ball back high in one hand and take a long stride forward into a balanced throwing position (figure 6-21A).
3. Pull the ball back past your head, extending your rear leg and rotating your trunk (figure 6-21B).
4. Follow through to give power and direction to the throw (figure 6-21C).

Figure 6-21

Throwing the Ball—Round Arm

This throw gives a longer range.

Teaching Points

1. Support the ball in two hands and look for a target.
2. Rotate your body, turning back toward the direction of the throw and cupping the ball in one hand (figure 6-22A).
3. Unwind, leading with your front leg and trunk and finally pulling your arm extended at shoulder level to release the ball (figure 6-22B).
4. Follow through (figure 6-22C).

Figure 6-22

Throwing the Ball—Overarm Bowl

This throw gives a longer range and a higher trajectory for clearing opponents.

Teaching Points

1. Sweep the ball back, cupping it in one hand and turning your body side-on to the direction of the throw (figure 6-23A).
2. Step forward into star position, push off your rear leg, and turn your hips and shoulders (6-23B).
3. Pull your arm straight past your head to release the ball overhead (figure 6-23C).

A   B   C

Figure 6-23

Punching the Ball

This technique is used for clearing the ball from the danger area when the goalkeeper is unable to collect it and he or she is being pressured by the opponents. The ball can be punched with both hands (figure 6-24A) or just one hand (figure 6-24B).

Teaching Points

1. Keep your eyes on the ball.
2. Use a one-foot takeoff to meet the ball high and as early as possible.
3. Contact the ball with your fist(s) flat and together, extending your arm(s) to follow through and direct the ball.

A

B

Figure 6-24

Punching the Ball Overhead

This technique is used to clear the ball with one hand when it comes in high over the goalkeeper's head.

Teaching Points

1. Go up to meet the dropping ball.
2. Swing your outside arm up and under the ball (figure 6-25A).
3. Contact the ball with the back of your hand and follow through to clear the ball behind your head (figure 6-25B).

A

B

Figure 6-25

Palming the Ball

Palming is used to direct the ball over the crossbar when the goalkeeper is unable to collect it or when he or she is harassed by the opponents. The palming can be done either with the outside hand (figure 6-26) or the inside hand (figure 6-27).

Teaching Points

1. Keep your eyes on the ball and watch it drop.
2. Take off with one foot, swinging your arms up for more lift.
3. Contact the ball with your palm and fingers as high as possible to direct it over the crossbar.

A   B   C

Figure 6-26

A   B

Figure 6-27

GOALKEEPING PRACTICE

In Threes

Drill 1: Out and Up

Player A plays the ball high to the goalkeeper, who picks the ball out of the air and throws it long (round-armed or overarm) to player B, who controls the ball and then repeats the drill (figure 6-28). Each player takes ten "crosses" from each side.

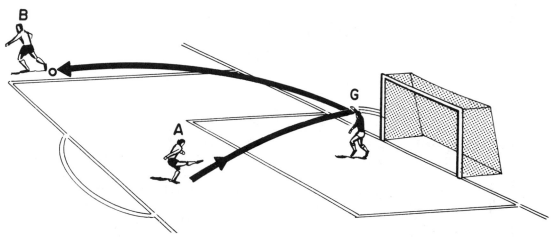

Figure 6-28

Drill 2: Reflex Drill

Two players throw balls high from the 6-yard line to give the goalkeeper the chance to sharpen his or her reactions and to use various handling and palming techniques (figure 6-29). The players should throw the balls for one minute, rest, and then repeat the drill three more times. They should keep score of the goalkeeper's contacts with the balls.

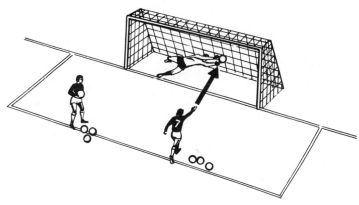

Figure 6-29

Drill 3: Punch or Palm

The goalkeeper challenges an opponent in the goal area for high balls. He or she tries to take the ball with two hands, but, if player B gets in the way, he or she tries to punch the ball clear to the side of the danger area (figure 6-30). If the "cross" is right on the goal line, the goalkeeper directs the ball over the crossbar with the palm of the hand. The goalkeeper takes ten crosses from each side.

Figure 6-30

HEADING TECHNIQUE

Heading in the Air

Heading in the air is necessary when the player must contact the ball as high as possible to head it into the goal or clear it before an opponent is able to intercept. (When the technique is first being learned, a lighter rubber ball can be used to improve the players' confidence.)

Teaching Points

1. Take a long last stride for a one-foot takeoff (figure 6-31A).
2. Arch your back in preparation for contact with the ball.
3. Contact the ball flat on your forehead (figure 6-31B).
4. Follow through with your trunk and neck, bringing your legs forward to compensate for the forward rotation (figure 6-31C).

A   B   C

Figure 6-31

HEADING PRACTICE

By Individuals

A tether ball (see p. 22) suspended from the crossbar provides an excellent coaching aid for beginners since it allows them contact with the ball on their foreheads and they can head the ball continuously.

Players can get the feel of the ball by simply throwing the ball up to contact with the head when it comes down. The next step would be for them to head the ball two or three times until they lost control of it.

By Pairs

The sensation of hitting the ball rather than being hit by it can be produced by having the students practice in pairs (the players could practice by themselves against a wall if there were no partners available). Initially, the player can hold the ball with outstretched arms and pull it onto the forehead to force it out of the hands. In this way, the player can concentrate on achieving the correct contact with the ball and sensing the striking of the ball. Here are four effective pair exercises.

1. One player throws the ball underhand to the other, who heads it back to the partner's feet for him or her to control.
2. One player sits down with legs outstretched and hands off the ground for balance. The partner serves the ball from a few yards away, and the player on the ground heads the ball back for distance, using neck and trunk action.
3. To practice heading for power, the player powerfully heads back a ball served by a partner 5 yards away.
4. The player practices heading for power as in exercise 3 but uses alternately a one- and a two-footed takeoff.

RECEIVING SKILL PRACTICE

Receiving from a Throw-in

From a throw-in, the OL feints to collect the ball and runs down the line (figure 6-32).

Figure 6-32

The OL, drawing the RB with him or her while moving to receive the ball, trap passes the ball back to the wing half (LH), who passes down the line for the OL to run on to (figure 6-33).

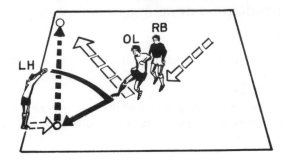

Figure 6-33

The IL runs to receive the ball from the LH but, instead of playing it back the first time, turns the ball around the opponent with the outside of the foot or allows it to roll through the legs and receives it on the run past the opponent (figure 6-34).

Figure 6-34

The OL fakes, collecting the ball on the wing, and comes back to take a shorter throw from the LH, creating a two versus one situation against the opposing fullback (figure 6-35).

Figure 6-35

Receiving from a Goalkeeper's Throw or a Goal Kick

The throw goes to the OL coming back deep to collect the ball, who receives the ball and plays it back to the LH or turns to create a two versus one situation against the opposing fullback (figure 6-36).

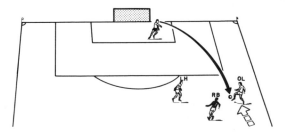

Figure 6-36

The forward practices collecting and turning the ball while being tightly marked (figure 6-37).

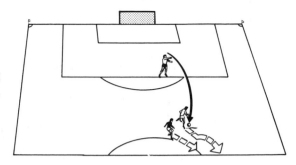

Figure 6-37

The attacking players use diagonal running and faking to receive the ball on the run and make space (figure 6-38).

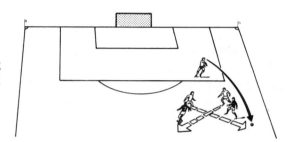

Figure 6-38

The OL runs as a decoy for IL, who collects the ball on the move (figure 6-39).

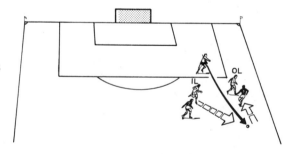

Figure 6-39

Receiving from a Corner Kick or a Free Kick

The receiver in this situation (figure 6-40) must control a hard-hit ball and shoot before being challenged by a defender, who is restrained at the goal line.

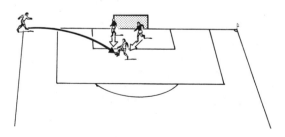

Figure 6-40

PASSING SKILL PRACTICE

Wall Passing

In this instance (figure 6-41), player A uses B as a wall to collect a return pass on the run as the defender is turning. If the feeder (player C) moves up quickly, then player A has an alternative—he or she can wall pass on either side (overlap).

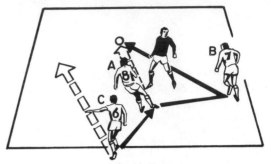

Figure 6-41

Setting Up a Pass

The feeder (player C) probes the defender's movements by playing the ball back and forth to players A and B (figure 6-42). They are setting up the situation so that they can determine what kind of a pass is "on," which depends on the movement of the defender (that is, to the receiver or to the space, in anticipation of another pass).

Figure 6-42

Triangular running and changing position are also effective in this situation (figure 6-43). The feeder passes and then runs to become a receiver, while the receiver takes the feeder's position.

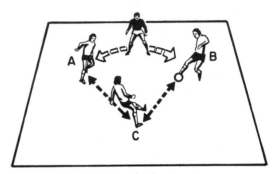

Figure 6-43

Through Passing

From a setting-up play, both receivers can break for a through ball (figure 6-44). The feeder selects the most penetrating pass.

Figure 6-44

Figure 6-45

Player C passes the ball to A, who sends the ball through to player B on the run (figure 6-45).

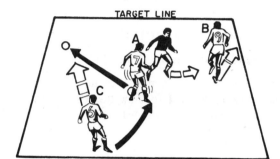

Figure 6-46

Player C passes to A, who fakes a pass to B and sends the ball through to the overlapping feeder (player C) (figure 6-46).

In a four versus two situation like this one (figure 6-47), the situation is still overloaded but, because of the confined area, the players need to use square passing, setting up, through and wall passing together with purposeful running. The target in this practice, apart from possession of the ball, is getting the ball through the defenders—trying to catch them lying square (in a line) in order to play through the space.

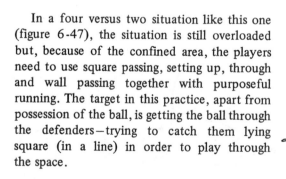

Figure 6-47

On the other hand, if the defenders are confined to the D arc on the edge of the penalty box, the alternative would be to release an attacker past them into the box (figure 6-48). The attackers force a defender to commit himself or herself by playing the ball to a marked player, who then effects a wall pass by passing the ball off the first time (one touch).

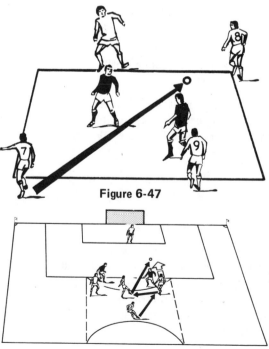

Figure 6-48

Then, by playing the ball in and back, the attackers can spread the defenders, leaving openings for a through pass (figure 6-49).

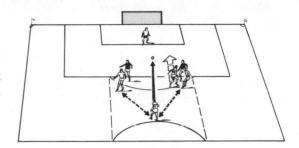

Figure 6-49

HEADING SKILL PRACTICE

Offensive Heading from a Throw-in

The LH throws to the OL, who heads the ball back to the LH to draw the RB forward. The OL then receives the ball on the run from the LH (figure 6-50).

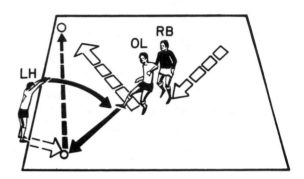

Figure 6-50

Offensive Heading from a Goalkeeper's Throw or Kick

The receiver of the goalkeeper's throw or kick heads the ball back to support the goalkeeper or deflects it to the OR (figure 6-51).

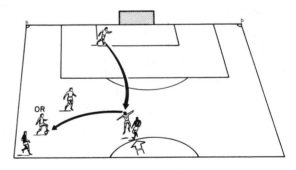

Figure 6-51

Offensive Heading from a Corner Kick

Figure 6-52 illustrates power heading for a goal from a corner kick. The ball should be played short, to the near post, so that the IL can come off the opponent and meet the ball on the move, arriving late but going at full speed.

Figure 6-52

Defensive Heading from a Throw-in

A throw-in goes to the forward. The defender, closely marking the forward, clears the ball by playing it out or to a target player, when possible (figure 6-53).

Figure 6-53

Defensive Heading from a Corner or a Free Kick

On a corner kick or a chip service, the defender heads the ball high, clearing it to a supporting player (figure 6-54). The heading defender should judge the run up to the ball and take off carefully to achieve good timing and power.

Figure 6-54

Defensive Heading from a Goalkeeper's Throw or Kick

When a player meets a throw or a kick from the goalkeeper, timing and takeoff are very important. The player should meet the ball high and play it down to a supporting player (figure 6-55).

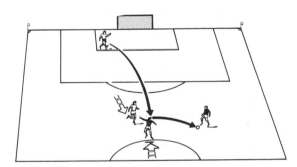

Figure 6-55

TACKLING AND DRIBBLING SKILL PRACTICE

These skill practices, conducted with opposition, support, and target, illustrate the players' correct responses to certain situations and give them practice deciding when to tackle. The tacklers' opponents receive good dribbling skill practice.

In the situation in figure 6-56, the defender is delaying the opponent in order to buy time until support arrives from the front.

Figure 6-56

Once the support is there in depth, the
defender can attempt to dispossess the attacker
(figure 6-57). The defender could use a front
block, a side tackle, or jockeying to try to get
the ball. Also, in this situation, the support
coming from the front could do the tackling
while the original defender dropped back to
cover. Collective tackling is often incorporated
into team tactics. If the ball carrier eludes the
first challenger, then the supporting player is
in a position to challenge.

Figure 6-57

The coach or teacher can make the opponent
hold the ball or attempt to beat the player
before shooting or dribbling the ball to the end
of the grid line or use some other means to
control the situation. In the same practice, if
the supporting player does not get back in time,
the defender is forced to tackle in a one-on-
one situation if the goal is in danger. If the
attacker moves at speed and takes the defender
on, the defender will have to use one of the
methods just described or, if the attacker moves
past the defender, one of the sliding tackles
(figure 6-58).

Slide tackling should be used as a last resort
in a dangerous situation.

Figure 6-58

Other players can be introduced into the
practice to create similar but more complex
defensive situations. A defender delaying two
attackers jockeys to create an interception
and to buy time for returning support (figure
6-59). The defender attempts to prevent
interpassing and to force the attacker down
the line, where there is less space.

Figure 6-59

The situation illustrated in figure 6-60 shows the rear defender's good balance. He or she is in good position to cover a through ball or closely mark the other attacker on a switch of play.

Figure 6-60

These tackling practices can be expanded to two versus two competitions across two grids (figure 6-61). The coach should watch tackling and dribbling techniques and principles; for example, he or she should point out that the attacker needs to commit the defender and draw him or her into an early attempt while the defender wants to delay and balance before attempting a tackle.

Figure 6-61

The situation in figure 6-62 shows penetration by dribbling, with mobility by the free forward destroying cover. Once the practices have been built up to three versus three or five to a side, the necessity of controlling the situation is apparent. The more passing opportunities there are, the less dribbling there is. To make sure that the players practice dribbling, the coach should insist that they beat at least one player before passing or dribbling the ball over the end line.

Figure 6-62

GOALKEEPING SKILL PRACTICE

The coach or teacher releases the opposition after starting the practice by throwing the ball to the goalkeeper, who collects the ball and throws it to the fullback (LB) (figure 6-63). The coach can feed the ball in different ways to control the practice, for example, by avoiding an opponent and finding a target player for a kick or throw. The opposition challenges the goalkeeper to perform efficiently.

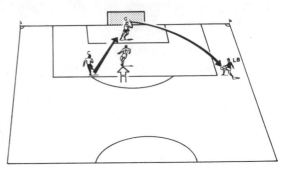

Figure 6-63

In the progression (figure 6-64), the fullback (LB) is covered, but there can be alternatives, with a link man (LH) or a forward (OL) coming back to look for the ball. The goalkeeper's throw or kick starts the attack. A small-sided game can be developed by giving the defense the target of passing the ball through the goal on the halfway line. It is important that the coach starts the game again after each goal with a service to the goalkeeper. Then, the goalkeeper's on-rushing opponent will make him or her react quickly.

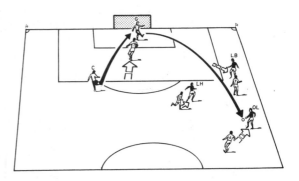

Figure 6-64

GAME-RELATED PRACTICES

Skills Circuit

The players rotate around the field in groups of three. At each station, they perform the practices outlined and change offensive and defensive roles. The goalkeepers remain in their goal areas at each end of the field. At station A (figure 6-65A), the goalkeeper throws the ball to the OR, who plays it back to the RH, who receives the through ball on the run up the wing to reach the halfway line. At station B (figure 6-65B), the OR fakes inside and then receives the ball on the run along the wing, reaching the goal line. The result of the maneuver is a hard-hit corner kick received quickly and shot at the goal. At station C (figure 6-65C), the winger leaves the LB to receive the throw and create a two versus one situation. The RH effects a wall pass to reach the target of the penalty box. The result of the maneuver is a hard-hit free kick received quickly and shot at the goal. At station D (figure 6-65D), a quick throw is received by the OR, who is coming back deep. The ball is played off to the IR, or a two versus one situation is created to reach the halfway line target.

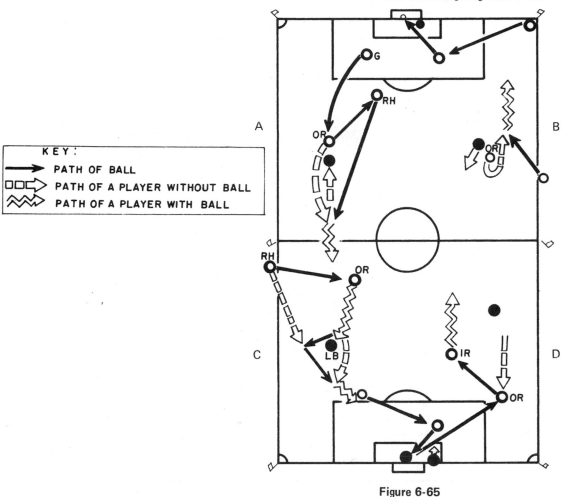

Figure 6-65

SMALL-SIDED GAMES

Attacking Game with Five versus Five or Seven versus Seven

This game puts the attacking forwards against a defense; two halfbacks who feed the ball to the forwards are introduced in this game. The offense should concentrate on intelligently building up the midfield with quick zoning and overloading of the defense when the fast break is "on" in order to take advantage of the situation and produce a scoring opportunity. In the situation illustrated in figure 6-66, various combinations of smaller situations and longer passing switch plays can be practiced in a realistic game situation. The passing combinations can be practiced by using only the players involved initially and then placing them in the game situation. Besides practicing passing in this game, the players can be coached on the principles of play and the tactics of both offense and defense.

Figure 6-66

Wing Play and Cut Back Ball

In this game, the RH feeds the ball to the OR, who has come back deep to receive the pass (figure 6-67). The OR carries the ball up to the IR, who has come up to support. The OR receives the return pass and goes to the goal line to cut the ball back across the goal area for any of the strikers to run on to and shoot. The ball can be fed left or right, so it is possible to have both wings practicing at the same time with two balls going.

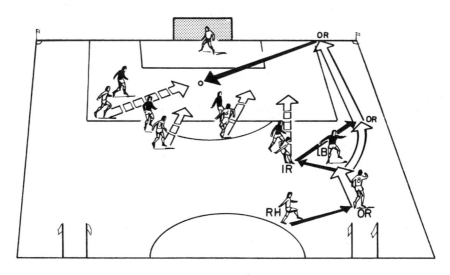

Figure 6-67

Setting Up and Through Ball

The LH builds up an attack in midfield by pushing the ball through to the CF, who comes to meet the ball, bringing the CH with him or her. The CF then sets the ball back to the LH, who pushes a through ball in for the CF or any other striker cutting in to run on to. If the CH isn't drawn out of position, then the CF has time to collect the ball, turn, and attempt to run with the ball or wall pass (figure 6-68).

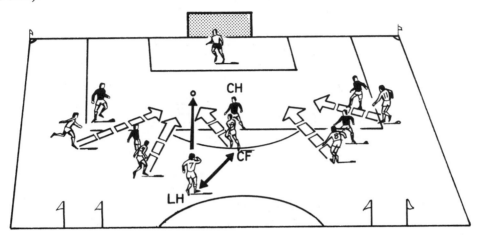

Figure 6-68

Switch of Play

The OR, having caused the defense to turn, feeds the ball back to the RH, who switches play with a long, crossfield pass to the deep-lying OL. The OL is in a position to collect the ball freely and attempt to wall pass or, in this case, cross a long ball to the far post for the strikers, switching play again and catching the defense on the turn (figure 6-69).

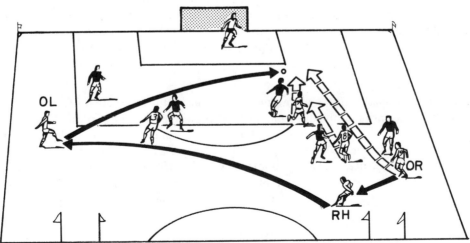

Figure 6-69

Decoy Running and Using the Long Ball

The OR runs as if to receive a pass from the RH, bringing the LB out of position. This leaves room for the IR or the CF to break into space on the wing to receive a long ball from the RH (figure 6-70). Decoy running can be used in many instances to create space between and behind the defenders.

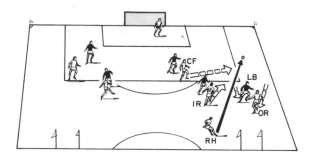

Figure 6-70

RESTARTS

Soccer, by its nature a fluid game, rarely lends itself to the use of set plays. Restarts, however, are the exception. In situations in which the play is being restarted, possession of the ball is everything. At a restart, attackers stand to gain increased penetration and possibly a goal. The defense is under constant threat and must be ready for surprises. The advantage to the attackers in corner kicks is generally obvious. The other restarts have traditionally been regarded as necessary only to get the ball back into play, and often neither side pays much attention to the offensive and defensive principles involved.

For the defense especially, set plays are crucial in restarts. No matter how unwilling a coach or teacher may be to use set plays in the offense, he or she cannot overlook the fact that the goal is threatened when the team is on the defense. Most coaches have definite opinions on offensive plays and how they can be combated, and some coaches believe in precise defensive drilling for specific situations. Repeated practice of restart plays can be very useful, but, rather than listing all the set plays here, the basic offensive and defensive principles in restarts will be reviewed.

Space

The creation of space affords more time for the successful completion of soccer skills. In all restarts, with the exception of the throw-in, the opposition is restricted by at least 10 yards according to the rules governing the restart. Therefore, the offensive team has an opportunity to use this space to its advantage. The defense will attempt to close this space as soon as the ball has been kicked in order to increase the chance of making an interception. In tight situations, the offensive team has to use increased skill since there is little space. But more important than the space in front of the defenders is the space between and behind them, which the attackers should try to take advantage of.

Movement

In order to create more space, intelligent movement by the offensive team is necessary; otherwise, it will be too easily covered. If the defense persists in player-for-player marking, more space can be opened up by using decoy runs. The tactic of covering zones or areas of the field rather than individual players may prove more advantageous to the defense, in which case the game will develop into a contest of mobility versus balance.

Selection

The onus of the offensive game falls on the player taking the restart. Depending on the space available and the possibilities created by intelligent movement, he or she has to decide who is in the best position to receive the ball. If the defense has prepared for the restart and retains its balance, despite the attempts of the offense to throw the players off, the selection should be limited and pose no immediate danger to them.

In addition to the principles mentioned above, the coach should analyze what principles of play are involved in each kind of restart and use this knowledge in the offense and defense to set up good plays for each situation. The next part of the discussion deals with the basic restarts in the context of these principles.

Kickoff

At the start of the game or after a goal has been scored, the team kicking off has an immediate advantage—penetration—and can capitalize on it. The offense should try to exploit any initial lack of depth or balance shown by the defense as it lines up for the kickoff. However, the kickoff involves more than just kicking the ball as far up the field as possible; there is no point in having the ball penetrate where there is no player going with it! After the ball has been put into play, when the offense has been able to pass it back to one of its players, the player with the ball should select the most penetrating pass. The pass will depend on the opponents' movement, whether they have lined up with poor initial balance or moved into vulnerable defensive areas or rushed toward the ball.

In the situation illustrated in figure 6-71, the fullbacks have been caught flat and close to the center line at the kickoff. The opposing forwards have rushed to intercept the ball at the kickoff, leaving space in midfield. If the offensive players move quickly toward those spaces, then the player on the ball has a number of good targets to choose from.

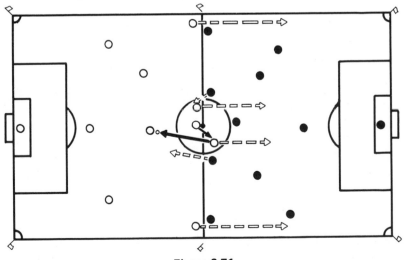

Figure 6-71

To stem this danger, the defense must maintain balance at all times. One player may be delegated the responsibility of rushing the ball in order to delay the penetrating pass while the other defensive players concern themselves with maintaining balance and adjusting to cover the penetrating runs of the mobile forwards.

Throw-in

When the ball is put out of play over the touchline, the game is restarted by a member of the other team, who throws the ball back into play. This rule of the game was invented as a convenient way to restart the game and give the nonoffending team possession of the ball. Many coaches, however, consider this a disadvantage for the team winning the ball because it is one player short (with one player off the field taking the throw) and the attackers can be closely covered to prevent their regaining possession of the ball.

The coach should recognize that possession and penetration are the priorities of the throw-in. In attack, players must remember the principles of mobility and improvisation to create sufficient space to receive the ball. They have one advantage—they cannot be ruled offside at the throw-in and, therefore, they can take up, or arrive at, advanced penetrating positions before the ball is served to them.

In defense, the defenders need to exercise great control and restraint to avoid being faked into poor positions, and they have to concentrate on maintaining balance in defense at all times. Here are some typical plays.

In the situation illustrated in figure 6-72, the forwards have created initial space by taking up position 5 to 10 yards from the thrower. In this way, they have created space to move forward and receive the ball since the defenders will normally take up positions between the player and the goal. The LH throws to the IL, who is covered but who passes the ball back the first time (one touch) to the LH. Possession is regained, and the LH is in a position to make another pass.

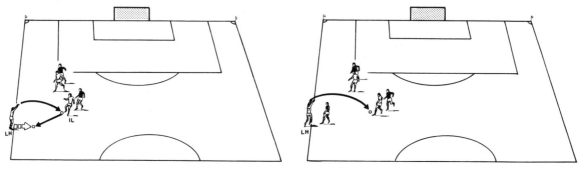

Figure 6-72   **Figure 6-73**

To counter the return pass, a defender could pick up the LH after he or she has taken the throw, since there is no restriction of distance from the thrower at the throw-in (figure 6-73).

In this way, the defense maintains its depth around the ball and has a one-on-one situation if the attack gets possession of the ball.

Movement

The more organized the defense, the more imaginative the attack has to be. Cover can be destroyed if players know when, where, and how to run.

There are many techniques for coaching players when to run. At the throw-in, the receivers normally take up stationary positions and then react with a quick burst of speed or a change of position at the thrower's signal (for example, bouncing the ball or slapping it with a hand). It is better for a player to arrive in a space late and move onto a ball at full speed than to arrive too early and be covered in a static position by a defender.

Knowing where to run can be taught by having players run in preplanned directions in practice, but generally players have to learn to react to different situations. They must be able to read the situation if they are to know the best places to go (into an open space to receive the ball or into a supporting position to allow someone else to receive it, for example).

In the context of a throw-in, the technique of running is important. Each player should be aware of the effectiveness of running *at* and *past* defenders to lure them into a decoy run and of running on the blind side of defenders in order to arrive in position without being covered.

The OL and the IL change positions, hoping to draw a defender with them. The thrower has to time the throw so that the ball is collected on the run. The OL draws the RB forward, creating space for the IL (figure 6-74).

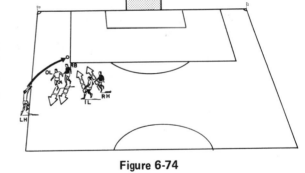

Figure 6-74

In this way, each defender will pick up the player who comes into his or her zone and can intercept when the ball is thrown towards him or her (figure 6-75). If the defenders fall for this ploy, they can be instructed not to follow the player but to play in a zone defense.

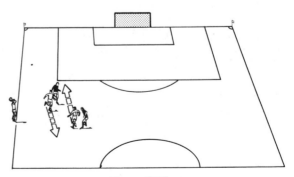

Figure 6-75

If the thrower selects the space between the defenders, the thrower's forwards will regain possession of the ball and have space to work in because of the defenders' immobility (figure 6-76).

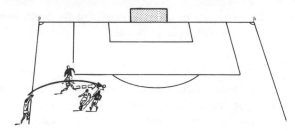

Figure 6-76

A free player in front of the thrower able to intercept the return pass or challenge the receiver for initial possession of the ball may be successful in combating the attack (figure 6-77).

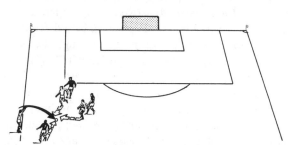

Figure 6-77

A sweeper or balancing defender at the rear may be successful in covering penetrating runs by the attackers (figure 6-78).

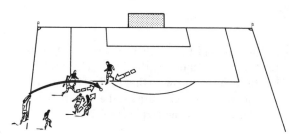

Figure 6-78

Selection

The influence of the players' movements on the thrower's selection of a target has already been illustrated. When the thrower has little choice, he or she naturally attempts to keep possession of the ball and build up an attack, but ideally the player will throw the ball to the player who has penetrated deepest and who is behind the greatest number of defenders.

Given the choice of safe possession with the OL or a penetrating throw to the IL, the thrower selects the more penetrating throw (figure 6-79).

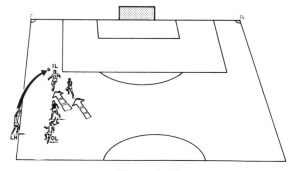

Figure 6-79

Against the threat of a penetrating throw, the defense may decide to cover just the most dangerous possibilities and sacrifice possession in less exposed areas of the field (figure 6-80). Rather than being drawn toward the ball, the RB is prepared to sacrifice possession in this instance in order to cover the penetrating IL, who constitutes a more dangerous threat.

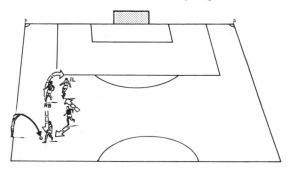

Figure 6-80

Goal Kick

By virtue of the fact that the goal kick is taken from the defenders' end of the field, it has not been regarded as an important restart from an attacking point of view. The most common kind of goal kick is one that sends the ball as far upfield as possible in order to put the ball into the opponents' half of the field and increase the chances of penetration and attack. Unfortunately, when little thought is given to the tactics of the goal kick, the defense can usually clear the ball since it is easier for defenders to head or kick the ball clear than it is for a forward to control the ball and turn with it. However, a long goal kick can be successful if it can be accurately directed to a target player upfield and teammates move into supporting positions.

In the situation illustrated in figure 6-81, the CF has created space by pushing too far upfield. From this position, he or she can move toward the ball from the long goal kick and pass it off into the open space for the supporting forwards to collect. If the CH gets to the ball first and clears it poorly, the supporting players can move on to it quickly.

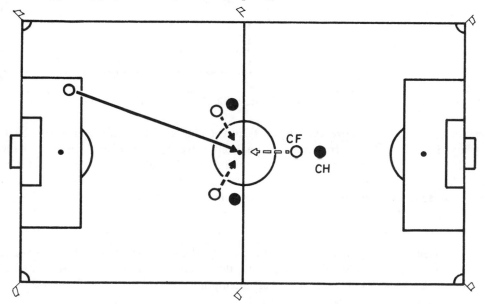

Figure 6-81

The short goal kick can be used to allow the goalkeeper more choice in distributing the ball. By passing the ball out of the penalty area to a defender, who gives it back, the goalkeeper has the choice of punting, drop kicking, or throwing the ball, depending on his or her preference or the range of the target. Often the goalkeeper is more accurate in throwing than in kicking, and many goalkeepers can throw the ball as far as they can kick it.

The desirability of penetration by putting the ball as far upfield as possible, however, is tempered by the possibilities of possession. A comparatively recent trend in the use of goal kicks has been to play the ball out short but safe to a player in the clear. This, coupled with the changing role of the fullback, in many instances has meant the use of this player developing, or being involved in, an attack from deep positions. In figure 6-82, the fullback receives a short goal kick and starts an attack by carrying the ball or passing it up to a forward.

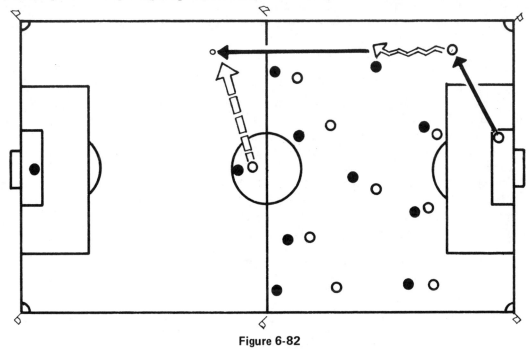

Figure 6-82

Defensive players should move aggressively against a long goal kick at the moment the threat first appears. They should meet any danger immediately since it is easier for them to clear the ball than it is for the offense to control it. It is important for the defense to keep in balance and to commit a player to challenge a short goal kick. Control and restraint must be exercised in attempting to challenge; this may be a way to obtain clear possession and start an attack.

Corner Kick

The corner kick has always been recognized as an important scoring opportunity. The ball can be kicked into the goalmouth from this restart. Often, the outcome of a corner kick is a battle of the giants, with a tall forward and a tall centerhalf attempting to head the ball. There are, however, many variations on the corner kick.

For example, when the kicker decides to use a long corner to kick the ball directly into the goalmouth, he or she has a number of alternatives. In figure 6-83, the ball is hit hard across the penalty spot. The forwards have withdrawn to the outside of the penalty box before starting their run. In this way, they create space to move forward into. By running in with determination, they will upset the defenders. If the first attacker misses the ball by jumping too early, he or she may leave a clear space for the next attacker to contact the ball.

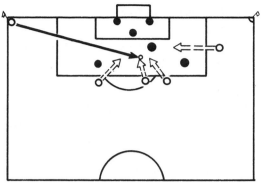

Figure 6-83

Coaching Points

1. The receiver of a corner kick should not start the forward run until the line of the ball's flight can be seen.
2. The run should be timed to arrive in the right space late but going at full speed. This is better than arriving under the ball and having to jump vertically in order to contact it, rather than forward and up.

Defenders have to counteract any mobility of the forwards by being mobile themselves. Otherwise, they are in a static position and at a disadvantage.

A variation of the long corner kick is playing the ball to an unmarked player outside of the penalty box, who can change the angle of the attack and perhaps try a long shot at the goal. The OL drives the ball deep to the LH, who in turn drives the ball back into the goalmouth (figure 6-84).

Figure 6-84

An in-swinging corner kick is often used with success to keep the goalkeeper in his or her area and to change the direction of the attack. The goalkeeper can be further troubled when awaiting the corner kick by a player positioned in front of him or her. This is not obstruction if the player moves away as the ball is kicked, and it often produces enough consternation to screen and unnerve the goalkeeper.

In figure 6-85, an in-swinging corner kick has been played to a target at the near post, who relays the ball back to a striker for a first-time shot. The goalkeeper has been worried by a player in front of him and is unable to reach the ball early enough to cut the cross out.

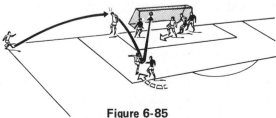

Figure 6-85

Often, a player in front of the goalkeeper will be able to score a goal from an in-swinging corner by being in a position to reach the ball before the goalkeeper. From the initial setup, many variations of the short corner kick can be worked out by changing the service. For example, in figure 6-86 no defender has covered the IL, who receives a short corner and takes the ball as close to the goal as possible before being challenged, at which point the ball can be either passed off or shot.

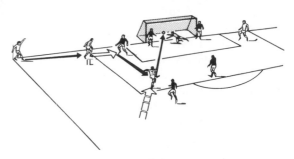

Figure 6-86

If a defender covers the IL, he or she has succeeded in utilizing the principle of width and has affected the concentration of the defense. But the defender can only come within 10 yards of the ball, so the IL can still safely receive the ball on the goal line. Then he or she can try to beat the defender or cut it back to an attacker. For example, in figure 6-87, the OL passes to the IL and then moves to receive a return pass going in on goal. If the attack succeeds in pulling two defenders out to combat the short corner, it has reduced the number of defenders in the area and the attackers may then take advantage of this additional space by playing a long corner.

Figure 6-87

Free Kick

The purpose of a direct or free kick is to get possession of the ball and penetrate. Following the basic principles, the attack will attempt to make space and the defense to cover any penetrating players and remain balanced. However, the closer to goal a free kick is awarded, the more advantageous and dangerous the situation is for the offense and defense respectively. The offense must decide at what distance it can launch a direct attack on goal, while, consequently, the defense must be aware of the range at which it becomes vulnerable. Generally, most free kicks inside the attacking half of the field can be kicked into the penalty box. Therefore, defenders have to watch out for attackers taking up advanced positions to receive the ball.

Depending on the caliber of play, a direct shot from the average player will not be a threat unless he or she is within the 20-to 30-yard range. There is no need to attempt to block a shot outside this range, but it is often a good policy to put one player 10 yards from the ball to prevent the kicker from using a low hard drive to a forward. The other defenders would initially take up balanced positions, marking player for player. The closer they are to the free kick, the tighter they mark the attacker, and the further they are from the ball, the more they cover the space.

When the kick is taken about 35 to 40 yards from the goal, the defenders have to maintain depth. The goalkeeper has the responsibility of coming out about 12 yards from the goal to intercept any long passes into the area (figure 6-88).

Figure 6-88

The defenders in figure 6-89 are marking players close to the ball tightly in an attempt to challenge a long quick pass. Attacking plays from deep free kicks have to be extremely accurate or very well timed to work.

A typical play is to attempt to drop the ball behind the defenders just outside the goalkeeper's range for a forward to run on to. This is a difficult spot to hit and most times is headed clear by a defender or picked up by the goalkeeper (figure 6-89).

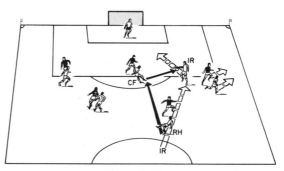

Figure 6-89

Fakes or dummies in free kicks are often tried, but to be successful from deep positions they have to be extremely well timed. For example, in figure 6-90, the IR fakes to take the kick but runs over the ball and keeps going while the RH passes the ball to the CF, who relays it to the IR, who is able to take the ball in stride and go in on goal.

Figure 6-90

The closer the free kick is to the goal, the more the defense will employ tighter marking and take up flatter cover. This will prevent forwards from taking up advanced positions while leaving the goalkeeper responsible for a 10- to 12-yard range from the goal (figure 6-91).

Figure 6-91

The use of a wall of defenders has become a common practice in blocking direct shots on goal. Each coach should formulate his or her own principles for the positioning and number of players and the method of setting up the wall from various directions. The following guidelines should prove helpful.

There are various ways to set up the wall, but many are inefficient or against the rules of the game. The most successful way is to line the players up about 6 to 8 yards from the ball in order to give a designated player (A) from behind the ball time to position a player (B) between the near post and the ball while the referee pushes the wall back another few yards. The goalkeeper moves to the far post to wait for the kick (figure 6-92).

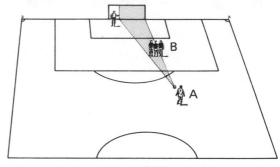

Figure 6-92

The number of players in the wall is decided by the goalkeeper, who constantly watches the ball. The wall of players is usually lined up between the shortest distance from the ball to the near goalpost. The player at the near post end is lined up a half-body width on each side of the post to prevent the kicker from shooting for the near post.

The goalkeeper usually takes a position just off to the center of the goal line toward the far post so that he or she is defending only half of the goal against a direct shot (figure 6-93). The wall is blocking the other half. If the ball is put over the top of the wall, then the goalkeeper has time to come across and intercept the ball. The theory behind this is that any ball shot over the shortest distance (near post) has to be lobbed, giving the goalkeeper more time to get to it. A direct shot over the longest distance (far post) can be watched longer and allows the goalkeeper more time to react.

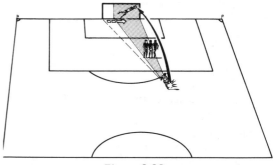

Figure 6-93

Opinions vary about the optimum number of players to have in the wall at various positions. Coaches may have their own ideas, but the goalkeeper should also be consulted. Here is a general guide (figure 6-94):

1. Four players for any free kick in front of goal in the area the width of the "D" — *never* split two players to each side.
2. Three players in the area from the edge of the "D" to the edge of the penalty box.
3. Two players in the area from the edge of the penalty box to opposite the 6-yard box.
4. One player in the area from the 6-yard box to the goal line.

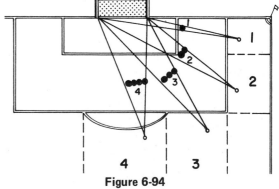

Figure 6-94

The offense's opportunities for attack against a wall of defenders depend on the improvisation of the attack and the efficiency of the defense. For example, the dummy run has to be extremely well timed and accurate to be successful.

In figure 6-95, the IR has run over the ball and is just onside when the ball is passed through to him or her by the CF, who has timed the run to get away from the CH and to receive the ball from the RH.

Figure 6-95

Various other combinations for releasing a player behind the defense can be worked out by the coach. Other attacking plays are for disrupting the defensive wall or blocking the goalkeeper's sight.

In figure 6-96, the attackers have formed their own wall beside the defensive wall in an attempt to block the goalkeeper's sight. The kicker has the option of chipping the ball over the defensive wall to the near post in the hope that the goalkeeper cannot see the flight of the ball until it appears over the defenders' heads. Another alternative is for the kicker to drive the ball at his or her own teammates, who break away at the last second. The idea is to surprise the goalkeeper, who may be anticipating a chip shot over the wall.

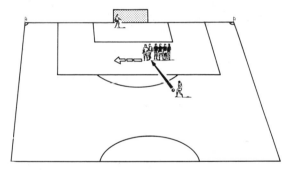

Figure 6-96

7

Level 3
Teaching Progressions

The third level in the teaching progressions for soccer concentrates on functional training, teaching the systems and principles of play, and conditioning methods.

FUNCTIONAL TRAINING

The functional training of a player focuses on some aspect of individual skill that the player has not been doing correctly or on some role in the game that he or she has been performing poorly. Almost all of the time spent on functional training should be spent on the individual players having trouble, although other players can be introduced into the training session to create a more realistic game situation. The basic principles to follow when the coach or teacher conducts a functional practice are the same three principles that have been followed on the previous two levels of teaching soccer: organization, assessment, and instruction.

When a coach or a teacher organizes a functional practice, he or she should:

1. Choose a realistic practice typical of the function or role of the player in an actual soccer game.
2. Always start the practice with a service to the player in order to focus on the player's function.
3. Outline the target or the aim of each function.

When the teacher or coach is assessing the needs of the players and their performance in a functional practice, he or she should:

1. Observe the outcome of each attempt.
2. Decide whether the success was the result of making the function too easy for the player.
3. Decide whether the failure was due to the player's lack of technique or to a wrong decision made under pressure (challenge).

When giving instruction in a functional practice, the coach or teacher should:

1. Restrain the opposition to give the player more time to execute the movement properly when the *technique* is poor.
2. Give the player more alternatives for success in the form of supporting players or a safety measure when the *decisions* the player makes are poor.
3. When the player is reacting efficiently, build up the practice to a completely live situation, perhaps a small-sided game, but still stress the function of the player who needs the practice.

In this way, functional training can incorporate all of the advantages of a skill practice rather than being just pure technique training. The coach or teacher should be careful not to increase the pace of the practice to such an extent that it becomes pressure training or mere conditioning, in which a breakdown of skill is likely to happen.

With these basic premises in mind, the coach can introduce and analyze the functions of various team members; the functions, of course, correspond to the roles of the players in the game itself. Some typical examples of the functions are described in the next sections; many others could be introduced in the same manner.

The Fullback's Functions

First, the fullback should be involved in a typical soccer situation so that his or her reactions can be observed. Figure 7-1 illustrates a situation in which the fullback (RB) is running back to control a through ball under pressure and then turns to find his or her target (the coach) with a long ball. From this simple situation, the practice could be built up to give the fullback more alternatives and, in turn, the alternative receivers could be covered in order to influence his or her decision so that the correct alternative is chosen.

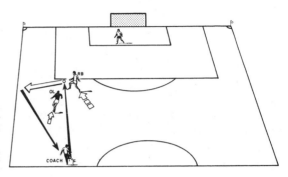

Figure 7-1

As shown in figure 7-2, the fullback, instead of running with the ball, can choose to play it back to the goalkeeper and to take the return throw on the run as an attacking fullback.

Figure 7-2

In this practice, the function of the goalkeeper and the function of the fullback have been linked together in *team play*. Of course, the goalkeeper would be covered with another opponent if the practice were continued and then the fullback would have to look to supporting wingers or link men. Here are some other situations that the fullback could be involved in:

1. Controlling the ball after chasing an overhead kick.
2. Intercepting a crossfield pass to the wing.
3. Balancing the defense, moving up to the wing man, moving back to cover against a through pass going past the centerhalf.
4. Dealing with a high cross near the goal.

5. Defending the goal line when the goalkeeper is out of the area.
6. Dealing with a two versus one situation.
7. Clearing volleys upfield and volley passing to a wing.
8. Attacking play with wing men and halfbacks.
9. Attacking at corner kicks and defending against them.
10. Taking throw-ins and defending against them.
11. Making low drives forward.
12. Placing free kicks.
13. Recovering and tackling again.

The Centerhalf's Functions

A centerhalf could be slow to make the correct skill response when under pressure. The player could be set up in a situation in which he or she could utilize techniques with support to improve the centerhalf's distribution of the ball.

In figure 7-3, the opposing forward is restrained outside the center circle to give the CH enough time to make the skill response (passing to a supporting player). As the center-half's skill improves, the opposition could be moved in closer to increase the pressure on the CH.

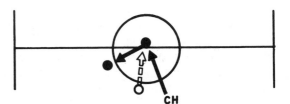

Figure 7-3

The following situations are also worthy of attention:
1. Heading from the goalkeeper's clearances.
2. Heading interceptions after corner kicks and high centers from the wingers.
3. Controlling a high ball followed by a clearance kick or a pass.
4. Handling passing situations—to the goalkeeper, a fullback, a halfback.
5. Recovering after a breakthrough by any forward.
6. Judging offsides.
7. Intercepting both setting up passes and through passes.
8. Chasing while being followed by tacklers.
9. Clearing kicks, volleying in a desperate situation.
10. Using accurately long, low drives to the center forward and wing men.

The centerhalf's awareness of the supporting players' functions and the nature of the whole situation will help his or her team play.

The Link Man's Function

The link man, or midfield player, is frequently called on to switch roles and to change from a role of supporting the forwards in attack to marking opposing forwards in defense. In a situation created to bring out this changeover function, the link man should learn to appreciate better his responsibility as a member of the *team*.

In the situation illustrated in figure 7-4, two players are playing against three. The link man starts with the ball, supporting a teammate in attack. If his or her pass is intercepted or a shot is saved by the goalkeeper, the ball will be quickly delivered to the opposing forward. The link man then has to think in defensive terms and chase back to challenge the opposing forward before he or she gets over the halfway line.

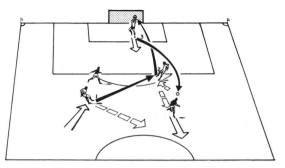

Figure 7-4

The practice could be developed further by adding a covering link man, and an understanding of offensive and defensive roles could be coached.

Other functions of the link man include:

1. Playing behind an inside forward or wing man, including setting up and through passes.
2. Positioning and breaking through for a shot at the goal.
3. Dealing with two versus one situations; covering against wall passes.
4. Dealing with throw-ins and corner kicks, both in attack and defense.
5. Linking with the other halfback during the first stages of an attack.
6. Servicing quickly for the forwards and crossfield passing.
7. Performing defensive heading near the goal.
8. Controlling the ball in tight situations.
9. Making short push passes—wall passing with a fullback, inside forward, or wing man.

The Functions of Wing Play

The function of wing play has become the consideration of all forwards and often of attacking defenders who "overlap" in this area of the field. The following functions of wing play should be practiced:

1. Committing the defender—techniques of dribbling.
2. Making the choice of moving to the inside or the outside of a defender (that is, right or left).
3. Performing defensive duties when possession of the ball is lost—chasing to delay or tackle.
4. Destroying cover by intelligent running when not on the ball.
5. Supporting the player on the ball.
6. Penetrating by blind side running.

In a three versus four situation like the one illustrated in figure 7-5, the wing player often has time to use his or her individual skill (in the functions numbered 1, 2, and 3 above) in a one-on-one situation. Deliberate encouragement of this ability should be incorporated into the function.

Figure 7-5

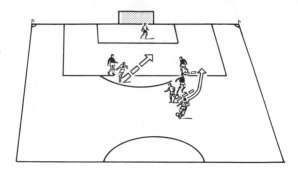

In the situation illustrated in figure 7-6, the link man decides to carry the ball forward while the winger attempts to destroy the cover by running in front of the two defenders and leaving space on the outside for the link man (functions 4 and 5).

Figure 7-6

By switching the ball to the center of the field, the defender may be caught turning (figure 7-7). If the winger moves when on the blind side of the fullback, he or she can receive a penetrating through pass on the run (function number 6).

Figure 7-7

The following possibilities can also be considered for functional practices:
1. Dribbling approaches to beat an opposing fullback.
2. Wall passing and through passing with an inside forward.
3. Running fast and center from the wing.
4. Moving inside, away from the touchline.
5. Making for the goal line and a low center.
6. Lobbing centers and fast centers from various positions outside the penalty area.
7. Volley shooting and heading from centers from the other winger.
8. Tackling an opponent a second time.
9. Taking throw-ins and corner kicks.
10. Controlling the ball from any type of service that may be expected in a game.

The Forward's Function

The primary function of forwards in soccer is to score goals. Apart from the skill practices covered in shooting and heading, players need to learn to recognize scoring opportunities. Too often, forwards want to make an extra pass in tight situations or simply look for a clear shot on the goal.

Practice with the three versus four situation (figure 7-8) in which the goal is being attacked stresses the basic principle of attempting to get a shot away at every opportunity in front of the penalty area. When the ball is forced out to the side, the players should keep possession of the ball and look for support.

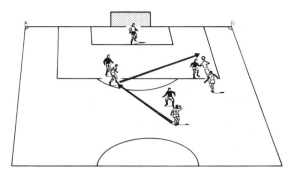

Figure 7-8

One forward can be selected for improvement in performance and the opposition can be restricted initially in order to give him or her success. Eventually, he or she will be exposed to the real situation, and all forwards should be aware of the following possibilities for recognizing and taking advantage of scoring situations.

In cut back ball (figure 7-9), if one forward succeeds in taking the ball to the goal line, the supporting forwards should anticipate the ball being cut back by timing their run forward to arrive at full speed, not getting there too early and being covered in a static position.

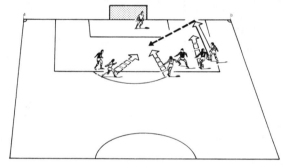

Figure 7-9

With the ball in the air (figure 7-10), after the ball has been played high to a marked forward, one attacker should go through, looking for a deflection, while the other supports from behind, looking for a poor clearance.

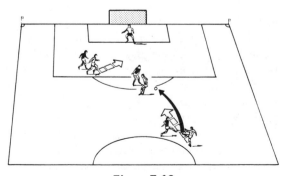

Figure 7-10

When the defense is set up for player-on-player marking, the two front forwards can open up the middle by intelligent running, which leaves a one-on-one situation by destroying the offense's cover (figure 7-11).

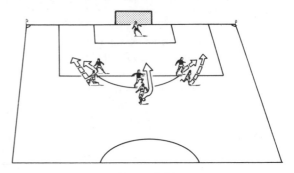

Figure 7-11

There are also many passing possibilities when player-for-player marking is employed, but forwards have to be coached in quick first-time passing to take advantage of tight situations.

1. Shooting and heading near the goal—a half-chance taken when under careful marking by an opponent.
2. Attacking with other forwards—three against two situations.
3. Moving to a wing position to receive a pass.
4. Controlling the ball when marked by an opponent.
5. Dealing with high clearances.
6. Using a setting up play to create space for other forwards.
7. Countering an offside plan.
8. Controlling the ball and screening in a confined space.
9. Running continuously and checking to escape an opponent's marking in order to receive a pass.
10. Running on an opponent's blind side to receive a pass; making a pass to a third player running on opponent's blind side.
11. Moving at throw-ins, corner kicks, and free kicks.

SYSTEMS OF PLAY

A system of play is simply a method of arranging players on the field in order for them to carry out particular duties. There are many systems to choose from. A failing of many coaches is that they impose a popular system on players of different ages, regardless of their ability and understanding.

The selection of a particular system of play depends on a number of factors, including: (1) the technical ability of the players, (2) their understanding of their part in the game, (3) the degree of fitness needed to execute certain systems, and (4) the system used by the opposing team.

The development of a system of play is a recognition of the strategic importance of space. By the specific arrangement of players on the field, coaches close dangerous space when defending and take advantage of open space when attacking. However, it requires a great deal of understanding on the part of players for them to be conscious of these strategies. Simply to put them in positions and expect them to emulate a successful system does not help them understand their roles in the game.

They need, first, instruction in the basic principles of play. This also gives the coach an opportunity to assess the ability of players in various situations. From this assessment, he or she should evolve a style of play that allows the players to perform to the best of their abilities.

It is not necessary that players learn the "labels" that the coach attaches to the principles but simply learn to recognize them and make the required movements intelligently.

PRINCIPLES OF PLAY

The principles of offense and defense are the foundations for the development of systems of play and other tactical considerations. For example, a basic consideration in the game is possession of the ball. In attack, the team must think and act positively; confident and accurate ball control are stressed, and the only justification for loss of possession is taking a scoring opportunity, that is, shooting. Conversely, when possession is lost, the team must think and act defensively, and repossession and safety are stressed.

From the basic principle of ball possession come the principles of offense (attack) and defense; offense depends on depth, mobility, penetration, width, and improvisation; defense on depth, balance, delay, concentration, and control/restraint.

The basic priorities of the game of soccer can be arranged according to the area of the field in which the play is taking place. Although a soccer field is officially divided into two halves by the halfway line, there are really three areas of the field that make up the strategic areas of play for the team in possession of the ball. For instructional purposes, the field can be divided into an attacking area, a midfield area, and a defending area, each of which takes up approximately one-third of the playing field. Figure 7-12 lists the priorities of the attacking team in possession of the ball according to the team's position on the field.

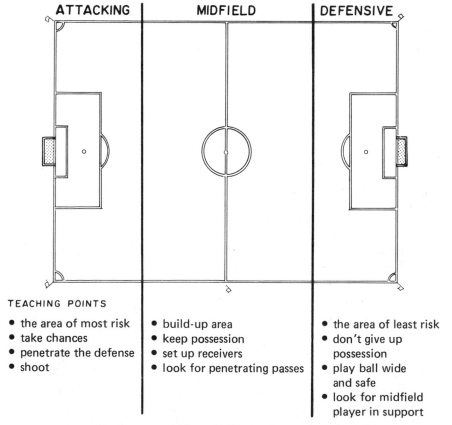

ATTACKING	MIDFIELD	DEFENSIVE

TEACHING POINTS

• the area of most risk • take chances • penetrate the defense • shoot	• build-up area • keep possession • set up receivers • look for penetrating passes	• the area of least risk • don't give up possession • play ball wide and safe • look for midfield player in support

Figure 7-12

Once the players have learned the three areas of play on the field, the coach should emphasize the two most basic and most simple principles of soccer: (1) "when our team has the ball, we will attack" and (2) "when the other team has the ball, we will defend." The simple principle of ball possession explains why the team should attack or defend but not how, so the principles can be further defined as (1) "when our team has the ball, we keep possession, we penetrate (go past the other players), we score" and (2) "when the other team has the ball, we block or delay their penetration, we prevent their scoring, we regain possession of the ball." These simple principles of play can be explained in more formal instruction based on the following principles.

Offensive Principles

Depth in Attack

Intelligent support of the player on the ball increases the number of passing angles and opportunities. The player off the ball (who is not in possession), must support or zone on the ball in order to give support and commit the opposition.

Players should realize that to have depth they must have support from behind and not be caught playing square or in a straight line since this limits their passing opportunities and increases the chance of interception by the opposition.

Figure 7-13 shows a situation in which there is poor support and no depth. Only square passing would be possible.

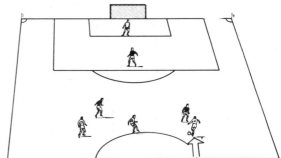

Figure 7-13

However, figure 7-14 shows good support, with intelligent running *off* the ball to increase the number of passing possibilities and to give depth to the attack.

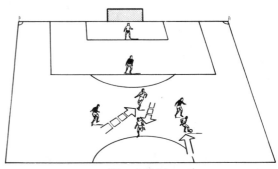

Figure 7-14

Mobility in Attack

At times all players, whether in attack or defense, must take on the roles of players around them. When a defender sees an attacker in trouble and moves up to support or overlap, he or she is showing mobility. Similarly, an attacking player may have to change position to cover for the overlapping fullback.

In the situation in figure 7-15, the RB goes on an overlap run, and the RH comes across to support.

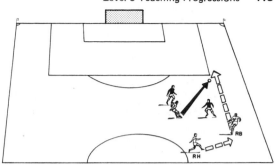

Figure 7-15

Penetration in Attack

Whenever there are two or more passing possibilities, the pass that achieves the greatest penetration should be used. The creation of goal-scoring opportunities and territorial advantage are the prime objects of penetration. The coach should assess the players' passing performance by looking at how many passes are going between or behind the opposition to create scoring opportunities. Or, are the attackers keeping possession safely and failing to go for the quick, penetrating thrust?

For example, the most penetrating pass in figure 7-16 is obviously number 3. It goes behind most defenders and creates a one-on-one situation, which can be overloaded quickly into a two versus one situation advantageous for the attack.

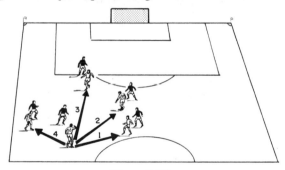

Figure 7-16

Width in Attack

Width in attack should stretch the opposing defense. This provides open space and, therefore, time for more passing situations. Lack of width allows the defense to concentrate in the most advantageous position.

The coach should set up waves of attack to emphasize the need for width. He or she should illustrate the effect on the defense and point out the increased passing possibilities.

In figure 7-17, the RB is controlling two players because the OL has come infield to an already congested area, making it easier for the defense to cover and possibly intercept.

Figure 7-17

Figure 7-18

In figure 7-18, the attack has been mounted in good width and both wingers have room to maneuver. As a result, they stretch the defense.

It is not only the position of the ball carrier that creates width, but the intelligent running of the other forwards.

Improvisation in Attack

The coach should set up a small-sided game (five against five) and stress individual skill and imaginative running by the players off the ball to create passing possibilities.

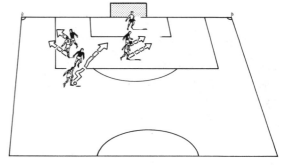

Figure 7-19

The supporting forward can draw off cover by running at and past the defender to let the ball carrier take on the opponent in a one-on-one situation (figure 7-19).

Defensive Principles

Depth in Defense

To combat offensive depth, the defense must limit the offense's passing possibilities by giving cover from behind. When defenders stand square or in line, there are innumerable passing opportunites and the attackers can easily penetrate the defense and perhaps score a goal.

Figure 7-20

In figure 7-20, the LH and the LB have been caught lying square and a through pass is open for the OR.

In the next situation (figure 7-21), if the LB observes the principle of depth, he or she will drop back. In that position, the LB could cover a pass to the OR or challenge the IR if he or she beats the LH. In this way, the LB could see both players and possibly anticipate their movements by intelligent positioning.

Figure 7-21

Balance in Defense

Depth around the ball is not enough, however. The defense must be balanced as well. A defense can have good depth in an isolated area and still be in a vulnerable position because it is not balanced. To counteract offensive mobility, the defense must maintain control of attacking space at all times. They can do this by adjusting across the whole field and not just in the immediate vicinity of the ball.

On the left side of the defense in figure 7-22, there is good depth but not on the rest of the field. There is poor balance on the right side since the players are standing in line with each other. Behind them is open space, which the offense can run into and use to create passing and scoring opportunities.

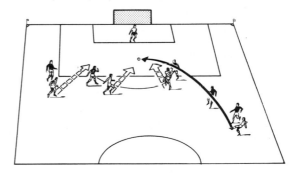

Figure 7-22

To demonstrate balancing the defense, the coach could set up four fullbacks and four forwards as in figure 7-23. The defensive players walk to their positions (for balance) when the ball is played out to one side. The fullback moves forward to pressure the attacker while the left centerback moves across to cover behind the left back. The right center-back gives cover and the right back balances the defense by lying deeper. Some coaches prefer to play this fullback in line, with the centerback restricting the forwards from more advanced positions. This tactic can lead to a flat rear line, which increases the chances of penetration on a through ball.

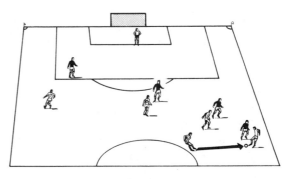

Figure 7-23

Delay in Defense

Delay is an essential principle of defense. On losing possession of the ball, initially the players nearest to it try to delay the opposition long enough to allow their teammates to reorganize. This can be achieved either by quick player-for-player marking of the players nearest the ball, with tackling and chasing by the forwards (which forces the opposition to use longer, more risky passes), or by backing off the player in possession and blocking the most decisive passing angle.

The coach should observe how well the forwards, in particular, tackle and harass their opponents after being dispossessed or beaten to the ball. The coach should illustrate the purpose of delaying and show them how they can use it in the game situation.

In the attacking situation in figure 7-24, the OL has just lost possession of the ball to the opposing fullback. The OL has chased the player with the ball back, limiting the passing opportunities and delaying the player in possession of the ball so that the returning defenders have time to run back and take up position again. *Delay = time = depth and support.*

Figure 7-24

Concentration in Defense

When the defense plays a tight player-for-player system, it is stretched by the width of attack and leaves huge gaps vulnerable to penetrating passes. The defense should funnel into the goalmouth and concentrate there. The idea is to limit the passing and scoring opportunities of the offense and to increase the possibilities of interception.

Figure 7-25 shows a defense running straight back, producing width in defense and leaving space for the attackers.

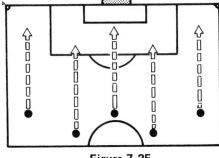

Figure 7-25

Figure 7-26 shows the defense funneling back toward the goal to close the space around the danger area by a concentration of defensive players around the goalmouth.

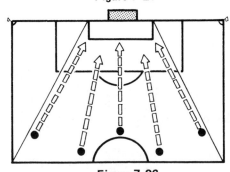

Figure 7-26

Control and Restraint in Defense

In all intercepting and tackling situations, the players must be confident, courageous, and determined if they are to regain possession of the ball. However, the defenders must exercise control and restraint, particularly when the opposition has the ball under control. When the defense commits itself wildly or too early, it may jeopardize the use of the other principles of defense and leave itself open for a penetrating attack.

The coach should watch out for the players' tendency to lunge into a tackle without regard for the tactical situation or the position of play on the field. The coach should illustrate the benefits of exercising control and restraint until the defense is organized and an opportunity to intercept the ball or tackle the ball carrier presents itself.

In the situation illustrated in figure 7-27, the LB has tackled wildly in a bad position, leaving the attackers with a two versus one option.

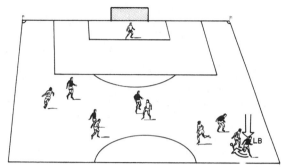

Figure 7-27

In the situation in figure 7-28, the LB has shown restraint by falling back as the opponent advanced in order to give his or her teammates time to get into a defensive position.

Figure 7-28

By teaching the players how to respond to general situations, the coach is, in effect, teaching players the tactics of a system that can be applied to isolated situations. Also, by observing players as they work on a principle, the discerning coach can select players who assume certain responsibilities naturally or are able to carry out specific tasks. In this way, players are picked for certain roles. The coach can base a pattern on the players' ability to perform specific functions within the team. Reinforced through functional training, a flexible pattern of play is allowed to emerge. Rather than lay down a set system, the coach should outline what certain players are expected to do within that framework.

Strictly speaking, systems are merely the labels and the numbers attached to various formations. The real value lies not in organization but in understanding the principles involved.

Only by practicing these situations can the players begin to recognize them in the game and accept the functional responsibility of their roles within the pattern of play.

Limiting younger players to restricted positions is as bad as attempting difficult formations and asking too much of them. The happy medium, of course, is allowing some freedom within the bounds of their duties. Usually, the younger the age level, the less need for complicated defensive formations and negative play. Aggressive, imaginative play should be encouraged, and all the players should have the chance to play their part in attacking the goal.

COACHING THE PRINCIPLES OF PLAY

Putting the principles of play into practice is a problem for every coach, but recognizing which principles are the ones critically affecting the game is a bigger one. If, however, the coach teaches by using opposites, he or she can contrast the principles of offense and defense, which helps the players understand the game better.

The grid (box) system of using confined areas for practice (see pp. 17-19) can again be used for teaching principles, and areas of the field can be marked off for setting up realistic practices, such as three versus one, four versus one, two versus one, one versus one, three versus three, three versus four, and five versus five. By using the grid system, the coach can restrict the space available and control the practice.

The coach can run the drills with an emphasis on using a variety of principles or he or she can teach a principle by selecting drills that illustrate one particular principle. An observant coach decides which point, of all the ones that might be taught, should be emphasized in a particular practice session. Then, the coach, emphasizing one principle at a time, would follow this procedure.

1. *Assessment:* The coach or teacher would have the class play five against five on half of a field (forwards versus defense) and demonstrate the principle or principles needing attention.
2. *Main Theme:* The coach would set up realistic situations (three versus one, four versus two, etc.) in a confined area to feature the principle. The situation could be built up by expanding the areas and introducing more players (three versus three, three versus four, etc.), still with the principle being stressed.
3. *Game Situation:* The principle would be practiced in a game situation (or the original practice of forwards versus defense) to work on the principle in a realistic context.

With this procedure in mind, the coach or teacher should look at the principles and the players and, when possible, try to set up realistic situations in which two principles (offense and defense) are in opposition. The coach should pose problems to the players and, while offering some guidance, observe how they solve the problems. In this manner, the next sections will deal with: (1) offensive depth and defensive depth, (2) offensive mobility and defensive balance, (3) offensive penetration and defensive balance, (4) offensive width and defensive concentration, and (5) offensive improvisation and defensive restraint.

Offensive Depth and Defensive Depth

Assessment: Depth in Attack and Defense

The teams should play waves of attack or five aside with no specific formation on either side. Support for the player with the ball in attack and zoning around the ball in defense should be the only emphasis. In the situation illustrated in figure 7-29, the defenders are showing good depth but the attackers are showing a lack of imagination in their positioning (7-29A); also, the defenders are too flat, leaving themselves open for a through ball and the attackers are executing a useful wall pass (7-29B).

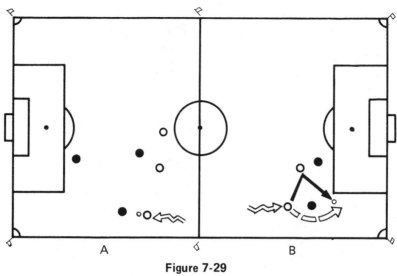

A   B

Figure 7-29

Main Theme: Depth in Attack

In the three versus two situation illustrated in figure 7-30, the attackers are showing intelligent running off the ball to give depth and thereby get support from behind.

Figure 7-30

In the three versus three situation in figure 7-31, there is good depth from the safety man in attack evident, with the forwards backing him or her.

Figure 7-31

In figure 7-32, a three versus four situation, the players are supporting the player with the ball from the front. Three players are confined to the box. They have to lose their cover in order to support the ball carrier and return a pass one at a time to prevent bringing the defenders to the ball.

Figure 7-32

Game Situation: Depth in Attack

The attackers are executing a setup pass and a through pass, and the LH is showing good depth (figure 7-33A). The RH is showing depth with a wall pass (7-33B).

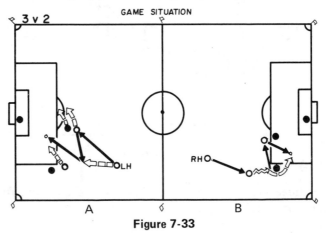

Figure 7-33

Main Theme: Depth in Defense

In this situation, two or more defenders constantly have to adjust their positions in order to give support and prevent through passing. In the three versus two situation (figure 7-34), the front player pressures the ball carrier, limiting the passing angle, while the rear player sweeps behind him or her to give cover support. If the rear player went to any of the other free players, he or she would be caught in line with the other defender and could let a penetrating pass get by.

Figure 7-34

In the three versus three situation illustrated in figure 7-35, good depth in attack is being countered by the depth of the defenders, who are giving cover support to the player pressuring the ball carrier.

Figure 7-35

Game Situation: Depth in Defense

In the game situation illustrated in figure 7-36A, the RB is in a position to watch the ball carrier and his or her opponent. By swinging behind the RH, the RB could give cover support. In figure 7-36B, if the LB moves forward to delay the attack, the CB moves across to cover and give depth.

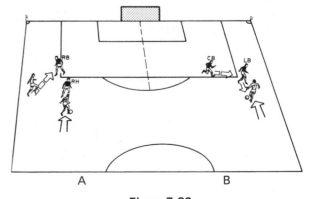

Figure 7-36

Application of Principles to Systems of Play

Herbert Chapman of Arsenal (the English first-division team) is given credit for developing the WM system in which the withdrawal of a central defender between the fullbacks closes the attacking space in front of the goal and between the defenders.

In attack, the WM shape (figure 7-37) naturally results in numerous triangular formations, which make it easier for players to support each other and maintain depth. The rigid adoption of this system results in player-for-player marking, with the fullbacks covering the wingers and the halfbacks covering the inside forwards. If a coach uses this formation, he or she should practice methods of attack and defense against a team using the same system.

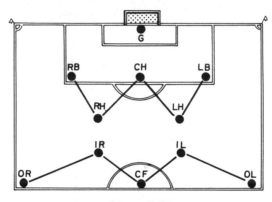

Figure 7-37

Offensive Mobility and Defensive Balance

Keeping set positions imposes player-for-player marking. Under these circumstances, in order to counteract this tactic, the attackers should use mobility to penetrate while the defenders should return balance to maintain good depth in all areas of the field.

Main Theme: Mobility

Passing practices with no targets other than keeping possession of the ball should be used initially since players need to learn how to interchange positions rapidly.

In the three versus one situation shown in figure 7-38, the attackers are using open and blind side running to create space and time.

Figure 7-38

When targets are set up on the end lines of the grid (figure 7-39), the players should be encouraged to play both in attack and defense. There is no set role that the players have to play other than running intelligently to receive the ball. One useful condition that the coach could impose would be to say that they may play the ball forward only. In that situation, they would have to be mobile in order to penetrate.

Figure 7-39

Game Situation: Mobility

In the situation illustrated in figure 7-40A, the fullback is overlapping and the IL is assuming defense duties, while in figure 7-40B the CF and the OR have exchanged roles.

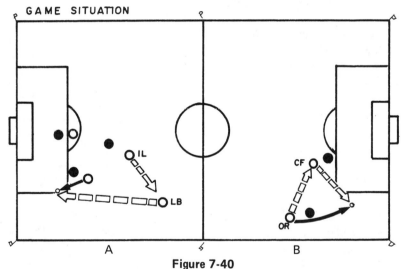

Figure 7-40

Main Theme: Balance

The defenders must react to a quick change of position by the attackers. They should know how to rebalance when the ball changes possession and is played past one of them. In the three against two situation in figure 7-41, when the ball is played past one defender, the other moves forward and they reverse positions.

Figure 7-41

Game Situation: Balance

If the defense has been using the conventional WM formation, the three-player back line would pivot around the centerback to give diagonal cover. This practice (figure 7-42) shows the movements required to rebalance the defense in the event of a quick switch of play across the field.

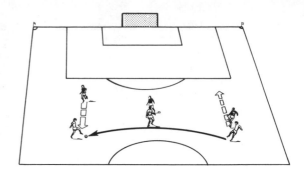

Figure 7-42

If the coach decides to use four rear defenders because of the threat of the more mobile forwards, the following practices should be conducted with the defense.

After a switch of play, the rear defenders pivot (figure 7-43).

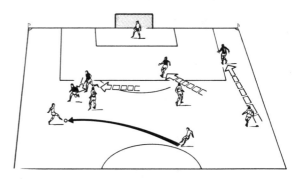

Figure 7-43

On a strike in the center, one centerback moves forward to challenge the attack while the other covers the space behind the challenging player (figure 7-44).

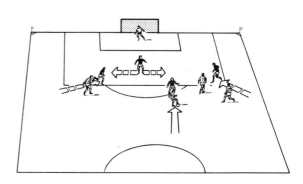

Figure 7-44

By contrasting balance and mobility in this way, the coach can develop the understanding necessary between players if they are to read the game intelligently and react. In attack, the coach should encourage intelligent, imaginative running and look for players who are prepared to run constantly. In defense, the coach should look for intelligent anticipation by the players and awareness in covering mobile forwards.

Application of Principles to Systems of Play

The interrelationship of these two principles of play directly affects the formation of players and their duties in the game. The effectiveness of mobility in attack was demonstrated to a great extent by the Hungarian national team in the 1950s. By withdrawing the center forward (as in figure 7-45), the Hungarian team attempted to lure the centerhalf out of the middle, and the inside forwards became the strikers in the spaces between the fullbacks.

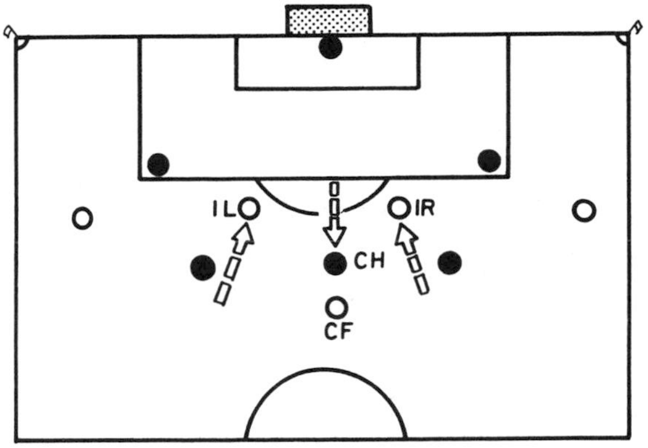

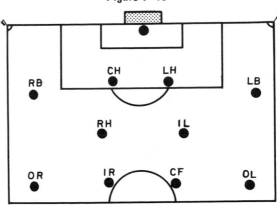

Figure 7-45

This defensive problem was combated by pulling a halfback into the rear line to play a four-back system (figure 7-46). This allows the two centerbacks to cover the middle area and, if one is drawn forward, the other covers at the rear. In this way, the defense attempts to close the decisive space between individual defenders in the rear line while conceding the space in the front.

Figure 7-46

This development, coupled with a four-player forward line, whose advantages were just then being recognized, led to the four-two-four formation.

Offensive Penetration and Defensive Delay

The eventual aim of attack is to penetrate the defense and score. Penetration in soccer is usually attempted at speed in order to catch the defensive players off guard.

Main Theme: Penetration

The players should look for the through ball or the penetrating pass. These are possible in situations in which the opponents are caught off balance and in line, either side by side or one behind the other. In the two versus three situation in figure 7-47, the offense uses a through ball rather than the safer square pass.

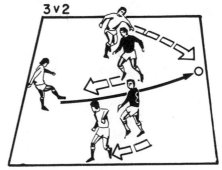

Figure 7-47

In this two versus two situation (figure 7-48), the attackers should play the ball early and as close to the defender as possible to prevent a wide run by the supporting player.

Figure 7-48

Game Situation: Penetration

In the situation shown in figure 7-49A, the attacker passes a through ball to the winger inside the RB. In 7-49B, the attacker uses a setup pass and a through ball with an exchange of position.

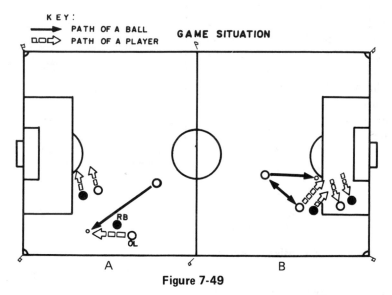

Figure 7-49

Main Theme: Delay

The player should practice in a situation in which he or she has to delay the opponent by narrowing the passing angles, showing restraint, and giving his or her teammates time to cover the opposition. In the three versus three situation illustrated in figure 7-50, the defender nearest the ball should be coached to pressure the ball carrier and cover support by his or her teammates.

Figure 7-50

When the ball changes possession, as in figure 7-51, a delegated player sweeps across midfield or midarea, attempting to intercept the ball or delay the attack.

Figure 7-51

Figure 7-52

In the two versus two situation in figure 7-52, the defender is attempting to delay the attacker by intellignet positioning to give the supporting player time to return from a deep position.

Game Situation: Delay

In figure 7-53A, the winger runs to delay the attack by the fullback. In figure 7-53B, the midfield link man becomes a sweeper in front of the defense.

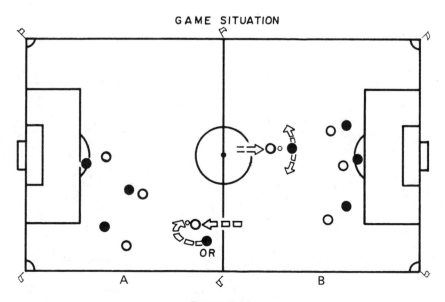

Figure 7-53

Application of Principles to Systems of Play

The principles of penetration and delay can be incorporated into any system a coach selects. It is simply a matter of persuading the players of the importance of the principles and helping them recognize when they should be employed in a game. Some coaches rely on a particular system to assist the team in using various principles.

A variation of the four-two-four system is this: withdraw a forward from the front line and use that player as a center midfield player to create a four-three-three formation. In that position, the player can further close the midfield space, which is exposed in the four-two-four system, and help lessen the intense demands on the two link men to delay the attackers. In the situation illustrated in figure 7-54, the three forwards have to use all of their attacking principles to succeed in penetrating. The use of an arrowhead formation overloads the two centerbacks. The midfield players can also be released to overlap in attack because of the cover given by the center midfield player.

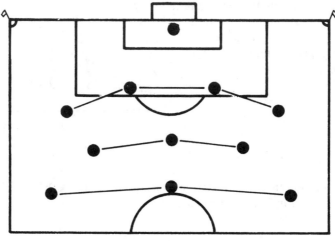

Figure 7-54

Offensive Width and Defensive Concentration

Main Theme: Width

The coach should illustrate the need for offensive width by setting up a tight situation. The players should immediately recognize success and failure. For example, in figure 7-55, it is obvious that at point 1 there are poor passing angles, although there is adequate space; and at point 2 there is less space and time but width has effected support. In the three versus three situation in figure 7-56, there is intelligent running off the ball to create width in attack.

Figure 7-55

Figure 7-56

Game Situation: Width

In the four versus three situations in figure 7-57A, the fullback overlaps, and in figure 7-57B the deep-lying winger (OR) passes wide to a player breaking quickly on the right.

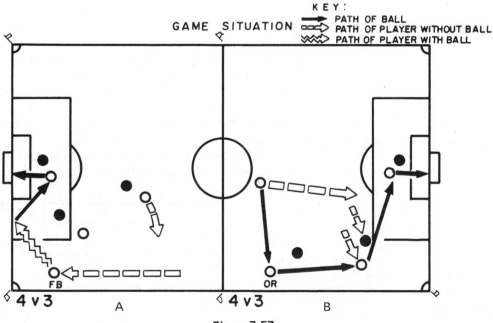

Figure 7-57

Main Theme: Concentration

The coach should set up situations with targets to give the players the feeling of funneling to close space. In the two versus two situation in figure 7-58, with the target (T) in the corner of the grid, the shape of the defending area makes funneling necessary.

Figure 7-58

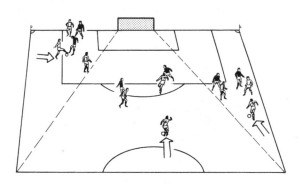

Game Situation: Concentration

In this practice (figure 7-59), the field is divided into the areas the defenders would normally play and three versus two situations are set up in each area.

Figure 7-59

Application of Principles to Systems of Play

Traditionally, the winger stayed out on the wing as wide as possible, ready to start an attack. Today, many systems of play use this wing, or flank, area in a similar way, but, stressing mobility in attack, it is not uncommon to find a fullback or a halfback going down the wing on what is commonly referred to as an overlap run.

Most systems that use four rear defenders use this tactic. The fullback knows that one of the centerbacks will cover from behind if he or she decides to go on an overlap. The danger of penetration from this area forces the opposition to concentrate in the vulnerable area around the penalty box. There are a variety of methods for concentrating and for reducing the space between and behind defenders.

The four-three-three system concentrates the defenders by playing them in rows. Another variation, the four-four-two system (figure 7-60), results from pulling the wingers of the four-two-four back into the midfield line when possession of the ball is lost.

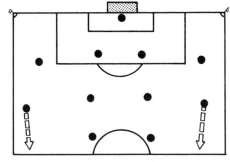

Figure 7-60

The sweeper used in systems of play is usually a free player who moves in from behind the rear defenders to "sweep" up any penetration of the defense. There are several variations on the sweeper formation. One of the centerbacks can play this role, for example, and in some cases the goalkeeper may opt to play a more active role in intercepting through balls that enter the penalty area (figure 7-61).

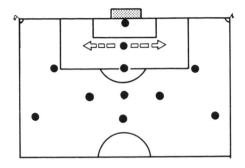

Figure 7-61

Offensive Improvisation and Defensive Restraint

The ability to do the unusual or the unexpected is becoming more and more necessary to successful offensive play because of the generally improved organization of defense in soccer. Success in attacking usually depends on individual skill, but using the principles and relying on the awareness of other players are also important.

Main Theme: Improvisation

In a situation like the one illustrated in figure 7-62, with one player against one player and with two targets (T), the ball carrier should be deliberately encouraged to use his or her dribbling skill. The coach should emphasize committing the defender by running hard, committing the defender to one direction, and changing pace and direction and faking to reach the target.

Figure 7-62

In figure 7-63, in a two versus two situation, the players should practice dribbling for penetration (with mobility by a free forward destroying cover).

Figure 7-63

Game Situation: Improvisation

In figure 7-64, the **RB**, having intercepted a pass to the winger, is able to carry the ball deep because of the cover given by the **OR** and the space-making runs of the other forwards.

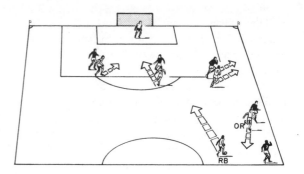

Figure 7-64

In a coached small-sided game, the players should be shown *how,* *when,* and *where* to run in certain situations in order to open up other possibilities. A dribbling condition of having to beat a player before passing should stress individual skill.

Main Theme: Restraint

The coach should set up situations in which the defenders have to time the tackle by "jockeying." This involves feinting, or pretending to challenge, while running backwards.

In the one-on-one situation shown in figure 7-65, the defender backs off and shows restraint until there is an opportunity to take the ball from the opponent.

Figure 7-65

In figure 7-66, the defender feints the tackle while attempting to cover the pass to a supporting player.

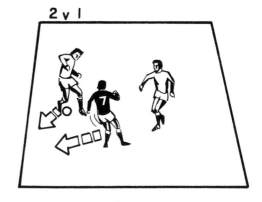

Figure 7-66

Game Situation: Restraint

In figure 7-67A, the defense shows restraint in setting up play, refusing to be drawn into a tackle. This gives the forward time to tackle back and help. In figure 7-67B, the retreating LB gives the defense the time to reorganize.

GAME SITUATION

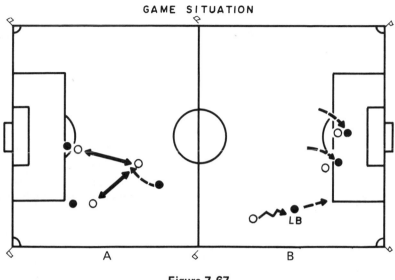

Figure 7-67

METHODS OF CONDITIONING

A review of the literature on soccer conditioning methods shows that there are many different schools of thought on the subject and a variety of methods for achieving fitness. The purpose of the training program that will be outlined in the rest of this chapter is to familiarize the North American coach or teacher with the current methods of conditioning and to discuss the benefits of each of the methods. Generally, every coach and teacher has his or her own ideas on fitness and tends to select those methods that are familiar.

General Physical Requirements for Soccer Players

Many training methods are based on tradition, personal opinions, or training methods used in other sports. Due to the lack of comparative experimental research in soccer, these methods can only be evaluated by means of already substantial research in the field of exercise physiology. By consensus, the physiological components of fitness that are judged important for playing soccer are: (1) endurance/stamina, (2) speed, (3) strength and power, and (4) agility/mobility.

Special Requirements for Goalkeepers

The goalkeeper requires special conditioning. Physiological studies have shown that the goalkeeper does not need as much general endurance training as the other players but that, in specific endurance, the goalie has more demands made on him or her during a game and needs special conditioning for specific endurance.

There is little point in subjecting goalkeepers to the amount of running that the rest of the players do. They don't need running speed; they need agility and reaction speed. To this end, they should be specifically trained to endure pressure. Probably more than any of the other players, goalkeepers should constantly be involved in live situations in which they are put under pressure. They should, of course, take part in warmup activities, but with special emphasis on the agility work. Circuit training and weight training are particularly applicable because of the short, explosive bursts of violent muscular activity characteristic of goalkeeping. Conditioning practices with the ball in competitive situations can also be adapted for goalkeepers by allowing them to intercept with their hands or dive on the ball.

ENDURANCE AND SPEED

Soccer demands stamina. Players have to keep going for ninety minutes, frequently sprinting, both with and without the ball. Physiologists call the ability to keep going at a moderate pace aerobic (with oxygen) exercise. The player replaces any oxygen used up as he or she is working on a pay-as-you-go basis. For example, a fullback falling back easily into defense when the opposition gets possession of the ball doesn't get winded.

The other kind of exercise is called anaerobic (without oxygen), meaning that a player often has to work for periods when he or she cannot pay back the oxygen being used up until he or she has finished working. For example, the fullback going on an attacking run receives the ball, reaches the opponents' penalty area but loses possession and has to sprint back into defense, arriving in position out of breath.

What does all this mean to the soccer coach? Simply that these two important factors must be incorporated into the training methods: first, the general endurance needed to keep going for ninety minutes and, second, the specific endurance required for short periods of maximum effort during the game.

Preseason training should concentrate on general endurance in order to prepare the players for the more intense demands of specific endurance. During the season, however, the major emphasis of training should be on specific endurance. This is not to say that general endurace should be neglected, but training studies have shown that the running involved in normal skill and scrimmage practices is sufficient to maintain fitness.

General Endurance—Preseason Training

Traditionally, soccer training consisted of continuous running or lapping of the field. This was done in the belief that the game demanded this type of long-distance endurance. Coaches eventually discarded it as inefficient. Even the marathon runners turned to other methods of training. Fartlek and interval training in athletics were adopted by soccer coaches as soon as the methods were developed.

Fartlek

Fartlek is a form of training featuring informal fast-slow running, as opposed to the formal fast-slow running of interval training. The pace should alternate between fast and slow, with a basic emphasis on fast running (preferably, although not necessarily, over natural surfaces such as golf courses and fields or through woods). This psychologically stimulating form of training, when properly executed, should develop both general and specific endurance in soccer players.

The activities listed below are just one example of the variety of exercises that could be included in a 2-mile fartlek. The players:

1. Jog ten minutes as a warmup.
2. Do five minutes of brisk calisthenics.
3. Run a half-mile at a fast, steady pace at about three-quarter speed.
4. Jog a quarter-mile.
5. Perform three or four acceleration sprints of 150 yards (jog 50 yards, stride 50 yards, sprint 50 yards), walking 50 yards after each.
6. Do four to six sprints of 20-50 yards, jogging 50 yards between each one.
7. Jog a quarter-mile as a warmdown.

This program should not be attempted at the beginning of the season. Such programs should be adapted to the players' level of fitness. A few players are usually capable of much more than the others. Youth soccer teams should concentrate practice over shorter distances, as in interval training.

Slow Interval Training

Slow interval training develops general endurance. Players run at a faster speed than in continuous fast-running training and are conditioned for more intense running. The heart beats at the rate of approximately 180 beats per minute during the effort, or fast, phase. Slow interval training is usually restricted to distances less than 880 yards. It includes repeated sprints of 100, 220, 440, and 880 yards.

The soccer field, which has a length of 100 yards, is perfect for 100-yard sprints. The players line up at one end line and their runs to the opposite end are timed. It is more beneficial for recovery for them to walk back to the starting point for the next sprint. The coach can blow a whistle at specific time intervals for players to gauge their sprint and recovery times.

During this initial phase, speed should gradually be increased and recovery time decreased in preparation for more demanding training. For example, one month of slow interval training would involve:

Week 1: A pretest of each player to ascertain his or her best time on a 100-yard sprint with a running start. Four or more seconds should be added to the player's best time. As an example, if the player's best 100-yard time is 12 seconds, his or her time for repetitions of the 100-yard sprint in slow interval training would be $12 + 4 = 16$ seconds.

The players should be trained to gauge the desired speed of repeats by the number of whistle blasts; for example, when they should be a fourth of the way, halfway, three-quarters of the way, and at the finish line. For a 16-second, 100-yard sprint, the coach would whistle at 4, 8, 12, and 16 seconds.

The players should build up their ability to run five to fifteen repeats at this pace, deciding for themselves when they are able to do more.

Week 2: The coach should impose more rigid time limits on sprint and recovery times. For example:
5 × 100 in 16 seconds with 60 seconds recovery. Walk 2-4 minutes.
5 × 100 in 16 seconds with 60 seconds recovery. Walk 2-4 minutes.
5 × 100 in 15 seconds with 60 seconds recovery.

Week 3: Time limits would be:

5 × 100 in 15 seconds with 55 seconds recovery. Walk 2-4 minutes.

5 × 100 in 14 seconds with 55 seconds recovery. Walk 2-4 minutes.

5 × 100 in 13 seconds with 50 seconds recovery.

Week 4: Time limits:

5 × 100 in 13 seconds with 50 seconds recovery. Walk 2-4 minutes.

5 × 100 in 12 seconds with 45 seconds recovery. Walk 2-4 minutes.

5 × 100 in 12 seconds with 45 seconds recovery.

Similar programs can be laid out for 200-, 440-, and 880-yard sprints. A running track is better suited for these, but, for the purpose of soccer training, the 100-yard interval is more easily organized and is more characteristic of the game.

Interval Training with the Ball

Many coaches also use game situations and running with the ball for fitness conditioning as well as variety. There has, however, been great doubt that these activities compare with interval training in terms of measurable speed and endurance benefits.

But recently, the Swedish physiologist Agnevik, who as investigating training with the ball, established that it produced the desired effects provided the activity was properly controlled. From his investigations came the following practices for developing general endurance.

Figure 7-68 illustrates a typical techniques practice: passing, receiving, and running with the ball inside a 20 × 10-yard area. It is also a good method for building stamina because it makes demands on the aerobic processes. The players make quick passes, run after the ball, and take up new positions, keeping this up for three to five minutes. After three minutes of rest, they go again for three to five repeats. However, the players must maintain a lively pace and continue to be motivated for the practice to be effective.

Figure 7-68

Three or four aside soccer played within a confined space (for example, across the penalty box) for two minutes with one minute of rest can be repeated three to six times, also.

Most players can, of course, continue these activities for much longer periods, but, if they are to gain the effects of interval training, the coach must put these time limits on the activities. The introduction of coaching points can be used to regulate the rest periods.

In the training practice illustrated in figure 7-69, two groups of four work alternately inside a confined area. One group works for fifteen seconds, each player running and dribbling with the ball, while the other group rests. The groups change over and repeat the practice.

Figure 7-69

Five aside soccer can be played on a full field for forty-five minutes. All of the players know how much stamina is demanded by five aside soccer on a full-length field. It is recommended that the game be played once a week to increase the players' endurance.

The practice in figure 7-70 is a two versus two situation played inside an area 10 X 30 yards, with another group positioned outside the boundaries. The object of the practice is to get the ball over the end line, but the players numbered 1, 2, 3, and 4 may assist the defending team. The groups change places after three minutes of work.

Figure 7-70

Dribbling practice can be done across two grids (figure 7-71). If player A can dribble past B, he or she then takes on player C. The object is to reach the far side of the grid. The sequence should be repeated for two or three minutes before the players exchange places, with B taking the ball and then C.

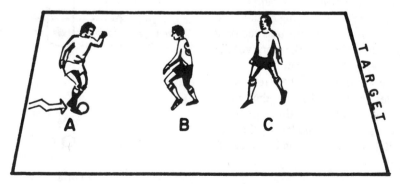

Figure 7-71

The practice illustrated in figure 7-72 is in diagonal running. Two players start at about 40 yards apart, one with a ball and one without. Zigzagging, they exchange the ball when their paths cross and they continue in this way down the length of the field.

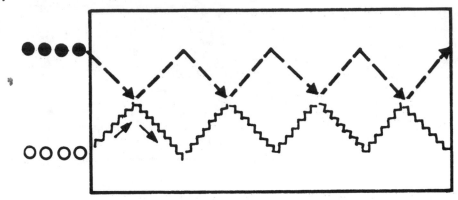

Figure 7-72

Specific Endurance—Competitive Phase

Fast Interval Running

During the competitive phase of the season, the pace of interval running should become more intense. In this method, players sprint all out for thirty to forty seconds. This activity simulates the kind of stopping and starting found in the game and promotes specific endurance. In order to place stress on the anaerobic processes, the corresponding rest interval is reduced from an initial ninety seconds to thirty-five seconds.

These training principles can be used in various patterns to simulate game conditions, and the inventive coach can devise his or her own practices to suit particular facilities and age groups. Here are some of the more common ones.

Figure 7-73 illustrates clock, or triangular, running. A number of markers are dropped around the center circle about 5 to 20 yards apart. The running pattern the runners are to follow should be specified, for example, the clock pattern of triangular running as shown in the illustration. If the coach uses colored markers or numbers, he or she can vocally instruct the players where to run. The players work for thirty seconds and then rest while their teammates work. Initially, the coach should work with groups of three or four. Later, the groups can be smaller so that the amount of rest between the runs is decreased.

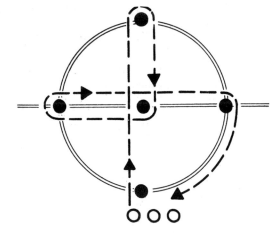

Figure 7-73

The maze run in figure 7-74 utilizes the markings in the penalty area. The players start at five- or ten-second intervals from a goalpost and they follow the route outlined by the lines of the goal area and penalty box. The total distance covered is 142 yards, which should take the players thirty to thirty-five seconds to run. After a minute's rest, the players can start running again. For motivation, the players can be started closer together and be given the object of catching the player in front of them.

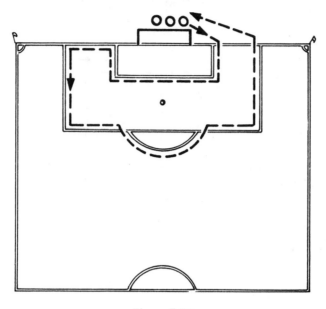

Figure 7-74

Sprinting around a 10-yard square, the players reverse direction when they reach the starting point (figure 7-75). They should run at full speed for thirty seconds, rest for ninety seconds, and then repeat the run three to six times.

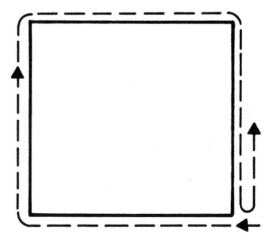

Figure 7-75

Relay races consisting of short sprints can be set up (figure 7-76). The 5-yard lines on a football field can be used, or markers can be dropped 5 yards apart on a field or a gym floor. Each player sprints to the first line, returns to the double line, sprints to the second line and returns, and so on. The total distance is 150 yards, which should be covered in about thirty or thirty-five seconds. The first player rests while the second player runs. At first, with three or four players on the field, each player will get sixty to ninety seconds of rest between runs. By reducing the number of players on a team, the coach can decrease the rest interval; the amount of rest should depend on the condition of the players.

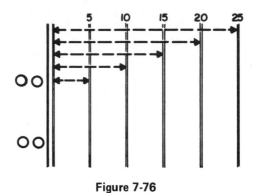

Figure 7-76

A lack of equipment need not handicap an inventive coach or teacher. For example, obstacle or maze running provides variety and competition when set up as a relay. It provides excellent training even if the players work hard for only thirty seconds. In the course shown in figure 7-77, the players can run in four-player relay teams through a maze using other players as the obstacles. The first player in each team sprints to the sideline, picks up a ball and sprints back, handing off to player number 2, who has moved up to the starting point. Player 1 continues to sprint, weaving between his or her teammates until reaching the opposite side line. On the return, player 1 has to leapfrog over and crawl under alternate teammates. When player 1 reaches the starting point again, player 2 starts to sprint and 1 goes to the back of the team. Many variations of this race are possible. With markers, flagposts, and even hurdles available in a school situation, much more variety can be brought into the race.

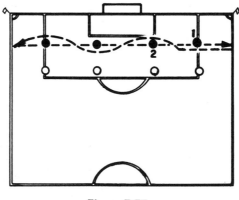

Figure 7-77

Interval Conditioning with the Ball

Again, interval training with the ball can be effective, provided that the players work for thirty to forty seconds at maximum effort.

In the training situation illustrated in figure 7-78A, two players are spaced 15 yards apart. They run and pass a ball back and forth over the length of the field. The ball should be played 10 to 15 yards in front of the players in order to encourage quick bursts of speed. The exercise in figure 7-78B is the same as the one in 7-78A, only the players receive, cross over, and run with the ball before making the return pass.

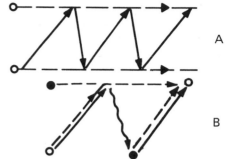

Figure 7-78

With groups of two or three players, the coach may want to incorporate some tactic or skill into this kind of conditioning. An extremely demanding practice with the ball is shown in figure 7-79. Two players are dribbling in a confined area. An efficient way of controlling the intensity of this practice is using six players working in groups of two. The object of the practice is to get the ball over the opposite end line and score a point or to make ten passes to the resting players before the opponent scores ten. While one pair is busy in the center, the other four players take up positions at each corner and assist in passing the ball. After ten passes, another pair takes over in the center of the grid.

Figure 7-79

The practice in figure 7-80 has players dribbling along a line in a coaching grid. The players practice feinting and dribbling skills with the defenders confined to their side of the line. The target (T) for the ball carriers is one end of the line. The players work for one minute and then rest for one minute.

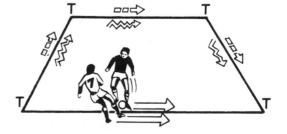

Figure 7-80

Pressure Training

Pressure training has been a popular training method ever since its introduction by Winterbottom. It consists of submitting a player to a series of ball services that come in quick succession. The player has to receive them by using a variety of techniques. The coach, of course, controls the practice by controlling the service. Winterbottom used it to improve skill. However, if the service is designed to cause maximum exertion over a short period of time, the practice can be used for specific endurance conditioning rather than skill improvement.

The following circuit format is recommended (figure 7-81). Some of the more common practices have been included, but others can be substituted by the coach when he or she wants to stress particular aspects of the game. The players should strive for a high level of success with the technique involved and work as quickly as possible. As in other practices with the ball, motivation is the key.

1. Players should work in groups of three or four, depending upon the group's degree of fitness. With three players, a player will work for thirty seconds and then rest for sixty seconds while the other two take their turns.
2. Players should move around as a group to the next practice.
3. They should always work in the same rotation for proper effect.
4. Players compete within their own group and with other groups for the best score.

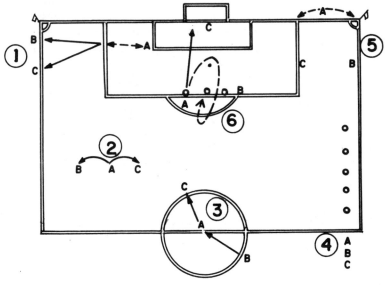

Figure 7-81

1. *Sprint and Pass:* Player A sprints forward 6 yards to meet a ball passed from B. He or she passes it first time to C and runs back over the line to where he or she started and then sprints forward again to meet a pass from C. The number of passes played in thirty seconds is the score.
2. *Heading:* Players B and C each have a ball and stand 10 yards apart, with player A in the center. Player A has to turn, jump, and head the ball back to each server alternately. The service should be quick enough for the ball to be in the air as A is turning.

3. *First-time Passing:* Player A stands in the middle of the center circle with B and C outside. B passes the ball to A and, at the same time, C calls for a first-time pass. C then passes back to A while B calls for the ball. B and C can move around on the outside of the center circle calling for the ball. The more time A takes to look for a target the fewer passes can be made in thirty seconds.

4. *Shuttle Run:* Five soccer balls are placed in a line, 5 yards apart, with the first ball 5 yards from the starting line. On the word *go,* A sprints to the first ball and dribbles it back to the start, turns, and collects the second ball, and so on. The number of balls he or she brings behind the line represents the total score.

5. *Receive and Pass:* Players B and C each have a ball and stand 10 yards apart and 5 yards away from the goal line. A stands in between them but on the goal line. When the drill starts, A sprints to receive a ball lobbed by C into the corner arc and passes it back. He or she then turns to sprint and receive a pass from B before it crosses the goal line and passes it back — repeating for thirty seconds. The number of passes made is the score.

6. *Shooting:* Player B places three balls on the edge of the penalty box inside the arc. Player C returns the balls from the goal. Player A has to run from outside the restraining arc and shoot a ball from the edge of the box and then run around the penalty spot and back outside the arc again before turning to shoot another ball. In this way, the player runs 20 yards each shot. The number of shots taken is the score for each player.

Pressure Training for Goalkeepers

The principles behind the pressure training circuit also apply to the goalkeeper's training. The goalkeeper may work in a group of players but substitute his or her own specialties at each station (for example, jumping to catch a ball instead of heading). The coach, however, may wish to train the goalkeeper separately and devise practices to strengthen in places where he or she is weak. Here are a few practices that are commonly used. The work-to-rest ratio is normally one minute pressure with one minute rest, with three to six repetitions for each drill.

Figure 7-82

In the practice illustrated in figure 7-82, the goalkeeper stands in goalmouth or in between two grids. Players on each side each have a ball. Goalkeeper takes a throw from one player, making a save, and then feeds it back. Immediately after, the goalkeeper turns to save a shot from the other player. The coach can instruct servers so that they stress fielding the ball at feet, waist, or above the head, diving to save, etc. A variation of this practice is to have the goalkeeper keep his or her back to the thrower, who calls "turn" when releasing the ball, making the goalkeeper react quickly to the flight of the ball.

Figure 7-83

In another practice, illustrated in figure 7-83, with the goalkeeper in center of a real or makeshift goal, the ball is rolled at each post by a player 1 yard away. The keeper has to scramble from post to post to stop the ball before it crosses the line. The number of contacts in one minute should be noted and compared to previous efforts to check motivation.

A variation of this practice is to move the opponents out to the 6-yard line and have them serve different kinds of balls toward the goalposts for the goalkeeper to collect and feed back again. Further variety (and exhaustion) is possible by making the goalkeeper start in various positions (for example, prone) before reacting to the ball. Or, he or she would have to perform forward rolls between each save.

STRENGTH AND POWER

Although certain exercises for certain components of fitness are stressed, a player should not be fit in one area and not the others. The coach has to consider fitness as a whole. Looking at the demands of the game in terms of speed and endurance, for example, he or she must recognize the importance of strength and power. In current strengthening programs for soccer, the most commonly used methods are circuit training and weight training.

Circuit training consists of carefully selected, simple exercises that are done around the perimeter of a field or a gymnasium. The circuit is suited to large numbers. Players proceed from one exercise to another without causing undue local fatigue but while working up to individual capacity. Progress is achieved, initially, by decreasing the time of performance and, later, by increasing the load, or the number of repetitions.

Circuit training is specifically recommended for the youth soccer coach who does not have the facilities for weight training or who has an age group (under twelve) that is too young for heavy strength training with weights.

The program should be included in preseason training to supplement endurance training, but it can be continued throughout the season. Initially, it should be used at the end of training sessions to motivate players to make a maximum effort.

Circuit Training Program

Done without any apparatus, circuit training makes use of the player's own body weight. Players can also train with light weights. The coach can vary the exercises and number of stations according to the apparatus available and the number of players involved. But, in organizing the rotation, he or she must consider the effects each particular exercise will have in terms of strain. The good coach avoids overloading any muscle group with strain by not running the same or similar exercises one right after the other.

The brunt of the exercises should, of course, fall on the legs, but consideration should also be given to abdominal and general body exercises. For example, a typical short circuit for soccer players might consist of this exercise sequence:

1. *Half-squat Jumps for Legs:* Player crouches until knees are at approximately an angle of 90°. (Players should not be encouraged to touch their heels with their hips since this can cause damage to knee joints.) From this position they drive up off ground and extend their legs in the air, landing in a crouch. Repeat.
2. *Push-ups for Arms and Shoulders:* Lying prone with toes curled for traction and hands placed below shoulders, the players push up. They extend their arms, keeping their bodies straight, and then bend their arms and touch their chests on floor. Repeat.
3. *Trunk Extension:* They begin in prone position, hands clasped behind neck. Keeping their legs still (a partner can anchor), they lift their shoulders and chests off the ground as far as possible. They lower themselves and repeat the exercise.
4. *Squat Thrusts:* From standing position, the players drop to a crouch, with hands flat on floor, thrust their feet backwards into a push-up position, jump back to a crouch, and stand erect. Repeat continuously.
5. *Sit-ups for Abdominals:* Player lies on back with knees bent, feet flat on ground, and hands clasped behind the neck; he or she sits up until the elbows touch the opposite knees.
6. *Shuttle Run:* The players sprint between two markers spread 10 yards apart, bending to touch the marker at each end as they turn.

Individual Training

There are various methods of conducting a circuit training session, depending on the age level and motivation of the group. One of the distinguishing features of circuit training is, of course, the fact that the coach can have each individual player work at his or her own rate and capacity rather than have all the players do the same number of repetitions. If this individual training is adopted, it becomes necessary to pretest each player's ability before establishing training loads. To pretest, the coach simply finds how many repetitions of exercises 1, 3, 4, and 6 they can do in a minute. For exercises 2 and 5, they should do as many as they can, with no time limit. To calculate training loads, the coach simply halves these results. This is the number of repetitions of each exercise the player should complete on the circuit.

A training session typically consists of three circuits done as quickly as possible. Retesting should be carried out to establish new training loads to see whether the circuit is being used regularly.

In school, players usually enter their training loads on an individual card and check their number at each station. This is difficult to do in the field unless the coach keeps the players' records and reminds them of their loads. The danger with poorly motivated groups, of course, is that players may do less than they should and simply go through the motions since each player is working at a different rate and it is impossible to supervise all of them at the same time.

Prerated Stations

A simpler method of organizing training loads is to specify average repetitions for each exercise. This method is not as individually beneficial as tailoring exercises to meet the needs of each player, but it proves to be a more effective way to motivate players.

In this procedure, the players are pretested, and depending on the range of scores for each activity, two or three categories (A, B, and C circuits or red, blue, and green circuits) of training loads are established. A card is posted at each station with the categories and training loads. For example:

```
PUSH-UPS
  A — 15
  B — 10
  C —  5
```

Based on their pretest scores, the players are assigned to training circuits — A, B, or C. In practice, the players complete the specified number of repetitions at each station but run three circuits as quickly as possible. Target times can be established so that, once a player reaches that target, he or she can move up to the next circuit.

Timed Stations

This is another method to cut out paperwork. The players work at each station for a specific time. They should be motivated to work as quickly as possible. In a typical session, the coach works them for thirty seconds and then has them move on to the next station and work there for another thirty seconds. The rationale for this is that stronger players will do more repetitions than weaker players in the same period of time, but players have to be motivated to do this. Care must be taken with younger or weaker players because, if the time is not properly limited, they may be achieving more than half as much as they did in the pretests, at maximum exertion.

Each coach has to decide which type of circuit works best with his or her players.

Weight Training Program

Only recently have soccer coaches begun to use weight training programs seriously. The traditional belief and fear was that this activity caused players to gain weight and, therefore, slowed them down. There is no physiological substantiation of this belief, however, and coaches are now recognizing the value of training with weights. Still, as in other sports, opinions vary concerning how to use them.

After getting into good general shape, the soccer player should begin the preparation program for strength training during the preseason phase. He or she may, for example, participate in circuit training for a few weeks before attempting to work with weights.

When the player has progressed to the set system of strength training, he or she can continue into the competitive phase of the season. Studies on weight training have shown the set system to be an effective way of training. This involves doing an exercise and then repeating it after a brief rest. The idea is to use a total amount of weight that would be impossible to lift without a rest. The set system develops the power necessary for endurance activities, such as pressure training.

Most coaches would agree that, working against light resistance, a player doing many repetitions can only improve muscular endurance and will not affect the amount of muscular strength. Weight training, or any other form of strength training, must include a few contrations at maximum or nearly maximum tension.

Studies on strength training indicate that three to nine repetitions a set are the optimum number of repetitions for building strength. The training program, therefore, requires the repetition, after a brief rest, of a few almost maximum contractions of the muscles involved in each exercise. The number of repetitions is kept low, usually about three to five for at least three sets.

Before embarking on a strength training program, the beginner should become familiar with the exercises and work into the strength program slowly. He or she should select a weight with which at least ten repetitions can be performed to practice the exercise. When the player is familiar with each exercise, weight can be added until he or she is only able to perform five repetitions. The player will then build up the repetitions with this weight until reaching a point where he or she is working with a weight that cannot be lifted more than five times.

Then the athlete can progress to the set system, attempting three sets of five repetitions of each exercise.

The following program of exercises provides specific strengthening of the muscle groups involved in soccer, together with general body conditioning.

Exercise Program

1. *Clean and Press:* This is a good exercise useful for warming up and strengthening. This exercise, done correctly, teaches the proper mechanics for all weight-lifting activities. The player begins by standing close to the bar, feet shoulder width apart and insteps under the bar. The player squats down, bending at the hips and knees with heels flat on the floor and back straight. The arms should be straight, gripping the bar just more than shoulder width apart. Then, the player drives the legs straight, keeping the bar close to the body while flexing at the elbow to support the bar at shoulder level (clean position). From this position, the player extends the arms to the stretch position overhead. He or she then returns to squat position by bringing the bar down to the chest, keeping it close to the body down to waist level. Keeping the arms straight, the player squats with the bar and returns to the starting position.

2. *Half-squats:* The players start as in circuit training—with the barbell behind their necks. They squat until their knees are at a 90° angle, drive up to straighten their knees, and bend to 90° squat again, and then repeat the exercise.

3. *Stepping:* With the barbell supported as for squats and with the flat of one foot on top of a standard gym bench, the player steps up, stands erect, and steps back down again.

4. *Dead Lift:* The player bends forward at the hips and grasps the bar, hands shoulder width apart. Then the player raises the trunk to the erect position, pulling the bar with straight arms to the thigh rest position. Then the player lowers the weight to the floor, and the movement is repeated.

5. *Heel Raise:* The player stands with toes and balls of the feet supported on a piece of a two-by-four, with the barbell resting across the shoulders. He or she raises the body up on the toes as high as possible and then slowly lowers the heels to the floor again.

This program should be followed three times a week, preferably on alternate days.

AGILITY/MOBILITY

The nature of the game of soccer makes the importance of mobility and agility obvious. Many training methods (the obstacle race, for example) stress agility, but attention should be paid to maintaining or sharpening this fitness component as part of warmup activities, which prepare the players for more strenuous activities.

Warmup

The warmup is important before all physical exertion and cannot be overemphasized, but it is often neglected in many sports. In a running game like soccer, in which great demands are made on the cardiopulmonary system and on other muscle groups, it is imperative that the body is prepared for the stress it will undergo during the game.

Torn muscles are the most common acute injuries suffered in soccer. Prevention consists of eliminating the possible causes: poor circulation, inadequate training, and cold. Muscular warmup, which must be a part of every athlete's routine, has an extremely important role in preventing injuries to the muscles.

First of all, some light running and jogging that raise the body temperature can be used. This should be done before the players engage in more strenuous running. The rule of thumb for the coach is usually to end the warmup when the players are perspiring and flushed in the face, but most coaches don't push hard enough in the warmup. However, after the running, stretching and agility exercises can be performed with less danger of muscle strain.

A variety of running activities, simple games, and exercises can be used during the warmup period. The ones that follow are just a few ideas.

Preliminary Warmup

The activities begin at a slow, jogging pace and follow this sequence. The players:

1. Jog 50 yards; repeat three or four times.
2. Jog, kicking one leg forward and upwards and then alternately. Repeat three or four times.
3. Breathe deeply in between each exercise.
4. Walk, circling arms.
5. Walk, turning the trunk and carrying arms across the body.
6. Jog, touching the right foot with the right hand and then the left foot with the left hand; repeat three or four times, with short walking sessions between each repetition.

After this preliminary loosening up, the activities should be done at a quicker pace. The players:

1. Running, touch the ground on the right side and then on the left side.
2. Running, go forward and turn sideways, both to the left and right.
3. Running, go forward and check to the left and then to the right.
4. Running, perform high jumps, with the arms reaching to the sky.
5. Running, do high jumps, heading an imaginary ball.
6. While running, do a knee raise and turn it outward with one leg, then the other, and then both.
7. Run, kicking the left leg across the body and then the right leg.
8. Run forward, turn, and kick left and right as high as possible.
9. Run forward, turn, run backward, turn, and run forward.
10. At speed and on command, touch the ground to the left and then the right.

One-Mile Continuous Warmup

The players, following the pattern illustrated in figure 7-84, run:

1. One lap of field in three minutes.
2. One lap of field in two and one-half minutes.
3. One lap of field in two minutes.
4. One lap, alternating between 50-yard sprint and 50-yard jog.

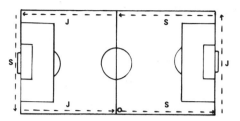

Figure 7-84

After the continuous warmup session, stretching and agility exercises can be performed with or without a ball.

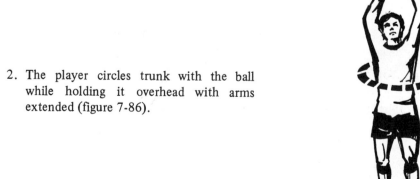

Exercises with a Ball

1. The player bounces the ball with both hands and jumps with the rise and fall of the ball (figure 7-85).

Figure 7-85

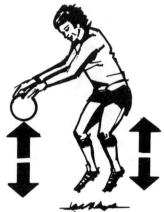

2. The player circles trunk with the ball while holding it overhead with arms extended (figure 7-86).

Figure 7-86

3. The player does a limbo twister, bending back and picking up the ball lying on ground either directly behind or slightly to the side (figure 7-87).

Figure 7-87

4. The player does hip circling. He or she circles the ball around the body while rhythmically circling the hips (figure 7-88).

Figure 7-88

5. The player moves the ball in a figure-eight around the thighs, raising each alternately (figure 7-89).

Figure 7-89

6. The player bends slightly forward to a straddle position and moves the ball in a figure-eight around the ankles. (figure 7-90).

Figure 7-90

7. The player bounces the ball with both hands while kicking an extended leg over the ball (figure 7-91).

Figure 7-91

8. While crouching, the player bounces the ball vigorously on the ground and jumps up to head the descending ball, go after the header, and control it instantly (figure 7-92).

Figure 7-92

9. Standing in straddle position, with arms extended with the ball overhead, the player swings down and tosses the ball in a high arc upward between the straddled legs and then turns and controls the ball instantly (figure 7-93).

Figure 7-93

10. Sitting with the ball in the hands, the player tosses the ball in the air, heads descending ball, gets up without using the hands, and controls the ball instantly (figure 7-94).

Figure 7-94

11. Standing in straddle position with arms extended and holding the ball overhead, the player drops the ball, turns, and tries to control it, using various techniques (figure 7-95).

Figure 7-95

Figure 7-96

12. Standing with arms extended and raising the ball high, the player kicks up and touches the ball, alternating feet (figure 7-96).

13. Standing on the right leg, with the knee bent, the player raises the left thigh, arms extended forward with the ball. He or she drops ball and flexes the lower leg to kick ball up to the hands, catch, and repeat while keeping perfect balance, alternating legs (figure 7-97).

Figure 7-97

Evaluation

In a soccer unit, evaluation of the students' progress and the feedback they receive from formal and informal testing programs are valuable parts of the learning process. Regular evaluations can be made by the teacher, by another student, or by the student alone by using the evaluation charts included in this chapter. The six evaluations cover wall volleying, juggling, dribbling, and heading techniques and the shuttle run as well as a general conditioning test, the 300-yard run. The students can be allowed to practice the tests throughout the unit and keep a record of their progress like the one illustrated in table 8-1, or they can be tested on a formal evaluation day at the end of the soccer unit. A test on the basic rules of soccer, to be given to students during level 1 instruction, is also included at the end of this chapter.

SKILLS AWARD PROGRAM

The results from the evaluation tests can be used in a skills award program* in which the students receive crests for achieving standards set for performance on the three levels: a bronze crest for achievement at the first level, a silver crest for the second level, and a gold crest for the third level. The standards can be set up according to the standards recommended in table 8-2, or the teacher can set up standards for students in the same school or class.

---

* The materials on the award program are used with the permission of the Soccer School Award Program. (See reference number 11 in appendix C.)

TABLE 8-1
PERSONAL PROGRESS CHART AND TEST RESULTS

Name ___A. N. OTHER_____ Age __10__

	Wall Volleying	Juggling	Dribbling	Heading	Shuttle Run	300-yard Run	Combined Award
Target Scores	24	5	16.0	5	15.0	63.0	
Individual Award	B	B	B	B	B	B	
March 15th	20	4	17.0	3	14.0	63.0	
Individual Award	—	—	—	—	S	B	
April 1st	25	6	16.0	7	13.0	60.0	
Individual Award	B	S	B	S	G	B	
Individual Award							
Individual Award							
Individual Award							

TABLE 8-2
RECOMMENDED STANDARDS

WALL VOLLEYING

Level /Age	7	8	9	10	11	12	13	14	15	16	17
Level 1	21	21	22	24	30	32	33	34	36	38	40
Level 2	24	24	25	29	35	37	38	39	40	42	44
Level 3	27	27	28	32	40	42	43	44	45	46	48

JUGGLING

Level /Age	7	8	9	10	11	12	13	14	15	16	17
Level 1	3	3	4	5	6	7	9	12	15	20	25
Level 2	4	4	5	6	7	9	12	16	21	26	30
Level 3	6	6	7	8	10	13	15	25	35	45	50

DRIBBLING

Level /Age	7	8	9	10	11	12	13	14	15	16	17
Level 1	22.0	20.0	18.0	16.0	14.0	14.0	13.0	13.0	12.0	12.0	12.0
Level 2	20.0	18.0	16.0	15.0	13.0	13.0	12.0	12.0	11.0	11.0	11.0
Level 3	18.0	16.0	14.0	13.0	12.0	12.0	11.5	11.0	10.5	10.0	10.0

HEADING

Level /Age	7	8	9	10	11	12	13	14	15	16	17
Level 1	3	3	4	5	6	7	9	12	15	20	25
Level 2	4	4	5	6	7	9	12	16	21	26	30
Level 3	6	6	7	8	10	13	15	25	35	40	50

TABLE 8-2 Continued

SHUTTLE RUN

Level/Age	7	8	9	10	11	12	13	14	15	16	17
Level 1	20.0	18.0	16.0	15.0	14.0	14.0	13.0	13.0	12.0	12.0	12.0
Level 2	17.0	16.0	15.0	14.0	13.0	13.0	12.0	12.0	11.0	11.0	11.0
Level 3	16.0	15.0	14.0	13.0	12.0	12.0	11.5	11.0	10.5	10.0	10.0

300-YARD RUN

Level/Age	7	8	9	10	11	12	13	14	15	16	17
Level 1	75.0	70.0	65.0	63.0	61.0	59.0	56.0	52.0	49.0	48.0	46.0
Level 2	70.0	65.0	60.0	59.0	58.0	57.0	53.0	50.0	47.0	46.0	44.0
Level 3	65.0	60.0	58.0	58.0	55.0	52.0	50.0	48.0	45.0	44.0	42.0

USING THE EVALUATION CHARTS

The six evaluation charts that follow are made up of a section of practice instructions, a section of testing and scoring instructions, and a table of standards. During the course of the unit, the students can be allowed to use the charts as guides for individual practice and they can take the tests and use the results to chart their own progress. Or, at the end of the unit, the charts can be used as the basis for formal evaluation. After they have been allowed some practice, the students can be tested individually and their performance can be recorded.

The instructions on all but the first chart are self-explanatory. The wall volleying tests in chart 8-1 were developed as tests on a single item that would measure soccer skill, and the Mitchell Wall Volley Test (developed by Reid Mitchell, "A Wall-Volley Test for Measuring Soccer Ability in Fifth and Sixth Grade Boys", an unpublished master's thesis, University of Oregon, 1963) and the Johnson Wall Volley Test (Joseph Robert Johnson, "The Development of a Single Item Test as a Measure of Soccer Skill", unpublished master's thesis, University of British Columbia, 1963) have been found to correlate closely with a player's proven game skill. The Mitchell test should be used for students twelve years old and under; the Johnson test for those thirteen to seventeen years old. The tests' dimensions should be marked out on the gymnasium floor and wall with tape, chalk, or paint according to the diagrams in figure 8-1, the Mitchell test (A) and the Johnson test (B).

Wall volley tests are also excellent training and conditioning aids especially good for use indoors during the winter months. Like the other evaluation tests, they can be used as a regular part of the students' individual practice programs.

EVALUATION CHART 8-1
WALL VOLLEYING

Find a suitable stretch of gym wall (indoors or out) or work with a teammate and try the following practices:

1. Practice inside of foot technique with ball stationary: step up to the ball; contact it with the inside of your foot turned flat to meet ball (slapping); and swing your lower leg through the ball.
2. Practice returning the ball first time (without stopping it) to a teammate or rebounding it off the wall. Build up to making as many returns as possible without losing control. Remember to lift your foot slightly to contact the center of the ball.
3. Practice getting behind the ball as it comes to you to play it the first time or control when it is bouncing awkwardly before using the inside of your foot again.

Test

Test yourself on the wall volley, and look up the standards for your age group.

Description

1. On command *go,* start test immediately. Drop the ball—it need not bounce before you play it against the target area. Continue to play ball to target area until the command *stop.*
2. You may use any skills. Play ball from behind line.
3. You may cross the line to retrieve the ball, but hits won't count. Use spare balls, if necessary, to save time.
4. Each ball striking the wall in the marked area and returning over the restraining line before *stop* counts as a hit and scores one point.
5. Three trials—total score.

Scoring: On the Johnson test: three 30-second attempts—total score. On the Mitchell test: three 20-second attempts—total score.

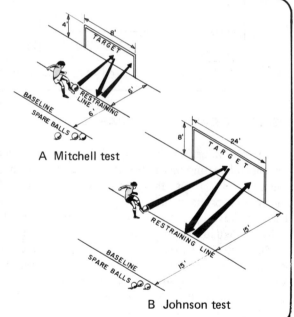

A Mitchell test

B Johnson test

STANDARDS

Level/Age	7	8	9	10	11	12	13	14	15	16	17
Level 1	21	21	22	24	30	32	33	34	36	38	40
Level 2	24	24	25	29	35	37	38	39	40	42	44
Level 3	27	27	28	32	40	42	43	44	45	46	48

EVALUATION CHART 8-2
JUGGLING

1. Drop the ball from your hands and allow it to bounce; then strike the ball once with your instep (laced area of your shoe) and allow it to bounce again.
2. Keep your toe back to make the ball go straight up into the air and just above your head.
3. Use left foot and then right foot, with one bounce of the ball on the ground in between.
4. Try to use your left foot and then your right with no bounce in between.
5. Try two bounces on your left foot with a bounce in between and then two bounces on your right foot with a bounce in between.
6. Practice until you can keep the ball up for two, three, and four touches until you reach your own personal best.
7. Use your thigh or upper leg for juggling by dropping the ball from your hands to make one, two, or three contacts with the ball before losing control.
8. Remember to contact the ball when your thigh is flat under the ball, not at an angle. Try for your record.
9. Start with your thigh again and, if you lose control, try to bring the ball back to thigh level with your instep.
10. Use your insteps and thighs to keep the ball in the air as long as you can. Try to beat your record.

Test

Test yourself on juggling, and look up the standards for your age group. To improve your score work at the practices before taking the test again.

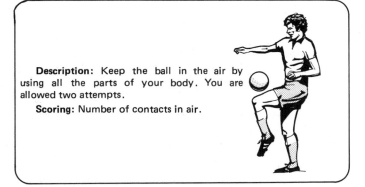

Description: Keep the ball in the air by using all the parts of your body. You are allowed two attempts.

Scoring: Number of contacts in air.

STANDARDS

Level /Age	7	8	9	10	11	12	13	14	15	16	17
Level 1	3	3	4	5	6	7	9	12	15	20	25
Level 2	4	4	5	6	7	9	12	16	21	26	30
Level 3	6	6	7	8	10	13	15	25	35	45	50

EVALUATION CHART 8-3
DRIBBLING

Practice your dribbling between six cones or markers set up 2 yards apart over a distance of 10 yards. Continue practicing to improve your record.

Test

Test yourself on dribbling, and look up the standards for your age group.

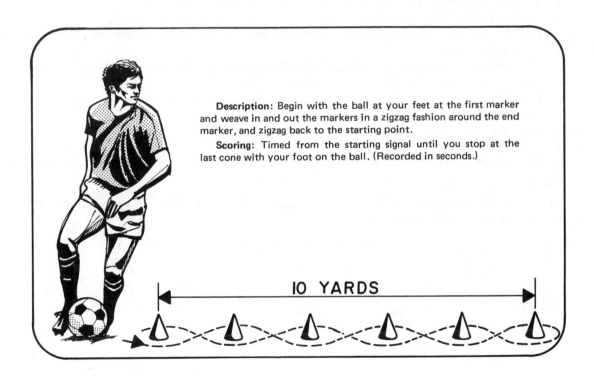

Description: Begin with the ball at your feet at the first marker and weave in and out the markers in a zigzag fashion around the end marker, and zigzag back to the starting point.

Scoring: Timed from the starting signal until you stop at the last cone with your foot on the ball. (Recorded in seconds.)

IO YARDS

STANDARDS

Level /Age	7	8	9	10	11	12	13	14	15	16	17
Level 1	22.0	20.0	18.0	16.0	14.0	14.0	13.0	13.0	12.0	12.0	12.0
Level 2	20.0	18.0	16.0	15.0	13.0	13.0	12.0	12.0	11.0	11.0	11.0
Level 3	18.0	16.0	14.0	13.0	12.0	12.0	11.5	11.0	10.5	10.0	10.0

EVALUATION CHART 8-4
HEADING

1. Hold the ball in two hands and pull it onto forehead, just above the eyes—this is your head contact with the ball.
2. Tilt your head back until your forehead is under the ball and you are looking straight up (keeping one foot in front of the other will help your balance).
3. Throw the ball up and contact it once with your forehead and then catch it.
4. Try two bounces on your head and catch the ball.
5. Try to move under the ball as you attempt your personal best.
6. Remember to head the ball upwards and not forward by moving under the drop of the ball each time you contact it.

Test

Test yourself on heading, and look up the standards for your age group.

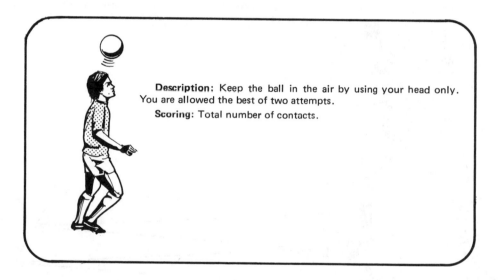

Description: Keep the ball in the air by using your head only. You are allowed the best of two attempts.

Scoring: Total number of contacts.

STANDARDS

Level /Age	7	8	9	10	11	12	13	14	15	16	17
Level 1	3	3	4	5	6	7	9	12	15	20	25
Level 2	4	4	5	6	7	9	12	16	21	26	30
Level 3	6	6	7	8	10	13	15	25	35	40	50

EVALUATION CHART 8-5
SHUTTLE RUN

1. Practice running with the ball at speed and then stopping it with the sole of your foot, right and left.
2. Contact the ball with the outside of your foot every stride over 10 yards.
3. Practice checking and going in the opposite direction by stopping the ball behind a line and sprinting back where you started from with the ball.

Test

   Test yourself on the shuttle run, and look up the standards for your age group.

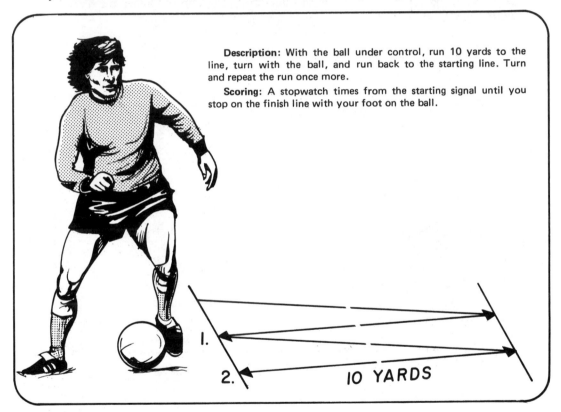

Description: With the ball under control, run 10 yards to the line, turn with the ball, and run back to the starting line. Turn and repeat the run once more.

   Scoring: A stopwatch times from the starting signal until you stop on the finish line with your foot on the ball.

STANDARDS

Level/Age	7	8	9	10	11	12	13	14	15	16	17
Level 1	20.0	18.0	16.0	15.0	14.0	14.0	13.0	13.0	12.0	12.0	12.0
Level 2	17.0	16.0	15.0	14.0	13.0	13.0	12.0	12.0	11.0	11.0	11.0
Level 3	16.0	15.0	14.0	13.0	12.0	12.0	11.5	11.0	10.5	10.0	10.0

EVALUATION CHART 8-6
300-YARD RUN

Build up your stamina for the 300-yard run by running repeats of shorter distances.

1. Run across the gym and touch each wall. Make five trips as quickly as possible. Rest for 30 seconds and then repeat until you can do this three times at full speed.
2. On the soccer field, sprint from the goal line to the edge of the 18-yard box and back three times. Rest and repeat twice more.
3. Touch wall at each *end* of the gym, making three trips as quickly as possible. Rest for 30 seconds and then repeat once more.
4. On the soccer field, sprint *across* the width of the penalty box four times. Rest and repeat once more.

Test

Time yourself on the 300-yard run, and look up the standards for your age group. If you wish to improve your time, try to improve your speed on the *practices* before trying the test again.

Description: Run a 100-yard course from the start to a 50-yard marker and return three times.

Scoring: A stopwatch times from the starting signal until you cross the finish line.

STANDARDS

Level/Age	7	8	9	10	11	12	13	14	15	16	17
Level 1	75.0	70.0	65.0	63.0	61.0	59.0	56.0	52.0	49.0	48.0	46.0
Level 2	70.0	65.0	60.0	59.0	58.0	57.0	53.0	50.0	47.0	46.0	44.0
Level 3	65.0	60.0	58.0	58.0	55.0	52.0	50.0	48.0	45.0	44.0	42.0

LEVEL 1 TEST ON BASIC SOCCER RULES

After the students have studied the basic rules of soccer (appendix B), they can test their knowledge of the game. They shouldn't be expected to memorize the rules, but they should be able to judge whether something is right or wrong. All of the answers to the questions are in the basic rules, and the students should be encouraged to go back over the rules to find the correct answers to the questions they got wrong on the test.

LEVEL 1 TEST ON THE BASIC RULES OF SOCCER

Place a checkmark in the correct box for each question.   True   False

1. A soccer field can be square in measurement.

2. The internal markings of a field can be adjusted for a small field.

3. When the ball goes over the sideline, the game is restarted by a throw-in.

4. When the ball goes over the end line, the game is restarted by:
   a. A goal kick—when the ball was last played by an attacking player.

   b. A corner kick—when the ball was last played by a defending player.

5. The penalty area indicates that part of the field where all players can handle the ball.

6. A goal kick or a free kick must pass outside the penalty area before it can be played.

7. A penalty kick is awarded for any penal offense committed by the defending team within the penalty area.

8. At a goal kick, all attacking players must be outside the penalty area.

9. Once the ball has touched the touchline, it must be ruled out of play.

10. The ball is in play when it is blown over the touchline in flight and then lands on the field of play.

11. When throwing in, the player must face the field of play and throw the ball from behind and over his or her head.

12. A player can be offside from a throw-in.

13. The basic difference between offenses meriting a direct free kick and those meriting an indirect free kick is a question of deliberate intent.

14. A direct free kick is given for a major offense; an indirect free kick is given for a technical infringement.

15. A player is NOT OFFSIDE when:
    a. He or she is not nearer the opponents goal line than the ball is.

    b. He or she is in line with the second-to-the-last defender.

    c. He or she steps off the field over the end line.

    d. There are two or more opponents nearer the goal line than he or she is.

Appendix A

Recommendation for Mini Soccer 7 Aside Rules

by North Shore Juvenile Soccer Association
British Columbia

The 7 aside program for Pee Wees has been proven highly successful in recent years by other soccer organizations around the world, including School Boy Soccer in England and FIFA sponsored groups in Germany, and also including juvenile clubs in both the Burnaby and Delta districts. Everyone involved in these programs is so satisfied with their success that they are convinced they are long overdue for the development of the game. The basic concepts are to encourage maximum participation in the play by each player (reduced numbers yields more touches of the ball, reduces bunching, limits sources of distraction, creates more open space for manoeuvring, and invites passing team work), to emphasize personal enjoyment (smaller fields and simplified rules of play makes the game more "fun", easier to learn, and less complicated to understand), and to reduce the competitive nature of the game as a team sport (elimination of team comparisons through awarding of points to game winners, publication of standings, and awarding of trophies emphasizes individual participation in the sport as a recreational game played for personal enjoyment, encourages development of individual skills, and detracts from the adult attitude that "winning" is everything and the objective to be achieved at any cost). These concepts of necessity envisage the scaling down to their own size of the traditional laws and environment of the game to more closely coincide with the age, stature, stamina and powers of concentration of small boys being introduced to a sport geared to older boys and adults. Many of the following rules have been proven successful. Others of them are either still experimental or entirely new, and for that reason are to be considered flexible and open for discussion and comment with a view to change. Please consider the rules and be prepared to discuss them at the forthcoming meeting.

The normal rules and laws of the game of soccer will apply subject to the following modifications where applicable:

1   Classification of league is identified by age, not division number, i.e. Pee Wee Age 6, Age 7, Age 8, and Age 9 (not Divisions 11, 10, 9 and 8). Age applies on or after January 1st of the year starting season. 6 = 1970; 7 = 1969, etc.

2   The programme is proposed for ages 6, 7 and 8 only, *not* for age 9 (age 9 presently being identified as Division 8) which age 9 league will play normal 11 aside standard Pee Wee rules as previously, including any 8's who request participation subject to available schedule.

3   Each player must be of the same age as all other players in the same league (i.e. ages 6 and 7 will not play together in the same league) with the exception as in No. 2 above.

4   Maximum number of players on field at any one time is 7, and maximum number of players per team is suggested at 11.

Reprinted with the permission of the Canadian Soccer Association.

5   The game to be divided into 4 periods of 12 minutes each, with a 1 minute break between 1st, and 2nd and 3rd and 4th periods and 5 minutes at half-time the re-start of play in the second period to be taken by the team that commenced the first, and the re-start of the fourth period by the team that re-started at the half.

6   Each player must participate a minimum of 50% of the total playing time.

7   Unlimited substitution, but during a stoppage in play only and upon the signal of the referee. Make use of 1 minute break.

8   No off-side rule to apply.

9   The normal throw-in rule to apply, with one re-throw allowed.

10 Regulation size fields not to be used, but if no other available the game will be played across the width of the field between the centre line and the goal line.

11 Regulation goal posts not to be used. Grass hockey goals an ideal size, but if not available marker cones or alternative to be used to delineate the goal area.

12 As to field markings, retain the traditional six yard goal area marking and eliminate the 18 yard penalty area marking.

13 The goal keeper cannot handle the ball outside the 6 yard goal area.

14 Steps will not be called on the goal-keeper who may put the ball into play within the 6 yard area either by place-kicking or punting or throwing including the re-start of play from a goal-kick.

15 The goal-keeper only is to restart play from a goal-kick or otherwise within the 6 yard goal area.

16 No goal can be scored by an opponent from a kick taken within the 6 yard goal area. To be allowed the shot must come from outside the semi-circle, and if it goes in off of an attacker it will not count, but will stand if it goes in off of a defender.

17 One coach or team official only to be on the field of play and not to stand or be within the 6 yard goal area during the course of play, and not to be behind the goal line. This applies to parents also.

18 Goal kicks may be taken from any point inside the 6 yard goal area.

19 Penalty shots to be taken from a 10 yard spot directly in front of the mid-point of the goal, instead of at the normal penalty spot of 12 yards.

20 The referee shall explain infractions to the offending players.

21 Coaches, managers, team officials and parents shall not criticize game officials at any time and shall encourage the same attitude amongst all players and supporters.

22 The ball to be considered "frozen" immediately the referee in his discretion considers that it is "in the possession" of the goal-keeper.

23 On the taking of a goal-kick no opponent to be closer to the 6 yard goal area marking than 10 yards.

24 The home team to line the field, supply size 4 game ball (leather if possible), be responsible for designating the goal area, supply the referee and avoid conflict in team colours.

Appendix B

Basic Rules of Soccer

FIELD MARKINGS

The size of the playing field can have an important influence on play. Because of the difficulty of obtaining adequate playing spaces, the rules of the game allow considerable variation in the dimensions of the field but stipulate that the length of the field must always be greater than its breadth. However, the internal markings on the field are always constant and follow this official plan.

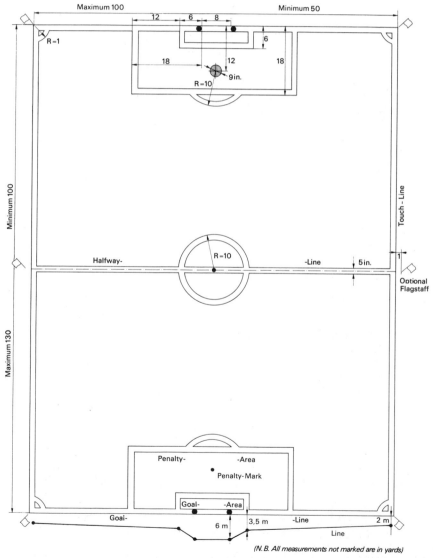

(N.B. All measurements not marked are in yards)

Touchlines (or Sidelines)

These lines mark the length boundaries of the field. When the whole of the ball passes out of play over either of the lines, a throw-in is taken by a player on the team opposed to that of the player who last touched the ball.

Goal Lines (or End Lines)

These lines are marked at the ends of the field, adjoining and at right angles to the touchlines. When the whole of the ball passes over the goal line (except between the goalposts and under the crossbar) either on the ground or in the air, the ball is out of play and the game is restarted by:

1. A goal kick—when the ball has last been played by an attacking player.
2. A corner kick—when the ball has last been played by a defending player.

When the whole of the ball has passed over the goal line between the goalposts and under the crossbar, a goal has been scored, unless otherwise provided by the rules. *Note:* The line itself is the outer edge of the marking; thus, all markings are within the areas they enclose.

Halfway Line

This line indicates a division of the field into two equal halves for the purpose of:

1. The kickoff—when all the players must remain on their own halves of the field until the place kick has been taken.
2. Determining offside—a player cannot be offside when in his or her own half of the field when the ball was last played.

10-Yard Center Circle

This circle, together with the penalty area (which includes the area within a radius of 10 yards from the penalty spot), provide practical indications of the rule that states that, for all forms of the free kick, whether direct or indirect, the players of the opposing side shall be at least 10 yards from the ball and shall not approach within 10 yards until the kick has been taken. The purpose of the rule is clearly to prevent interference with free kicks, as well as place kicks, goal kicks, and corner kicks. *Note:* The above rule—10 yards away from the ball —applies to opposing players standing behind the ball as well as those in front of it, except in these three cases:

1. For a penalty kick, all the players other than the goalkeeper and the player taking the kick must be outside the penalty area within the field of play and 10 yards from the ball at the time the kick is taken; the goalkeeper must stand on the goal line between the goalposts.
2. At a goal kick, all attacking players must be outside the penalty area.
3. When an indirect free kick is awarded in the penalty area but less than 10 yards from the goal line, the defending players are allowed to stand on the goal line between the posts.

Penalty Area

This area is a rectangle 44 yards by 18 yards (including the width of the line). It serves the following purposes:

1. It indicates that part of the field in which any of the nine penal offenses committed intentionally by a defending player result in the awarding of a penalty kick.

2. It indicates the part of the field in which the goalkeeper is allowed to handle the ball.
3. It indicates the distance the ball must be kicked from the goal area when a goal kick, or a free kick awarded to the defending side, is taken before the ball is deemed to be in play (that is, before it can be played by another player).
4. When a penalty kick is awarded, the penalty area indicates the area outside of which all the players other than the goalkeeper and the player taking the penalty kick must stand on the field of play or outside of which all opposing players must remain while a goal kick is being taken.

The penalty arc is not part of the penalty area; it is only the marking that indicates the distance of 10 yards from the penalty spot when a penalty kick is being taken. For a penalty, the ball is placed on the penalty spot, which is approximately 9 inches in diameter and which is marked on the field 12 yards from the center of the goal line between the goalposts.

Goal Area

The goal area has two purposes:

1. It indicates the area in which the goalkeeper has special protection (he or she can only be charged when he or she is in possession of the ball or obstructing an opponent).
2. It limits the area in which the ball is placed for a goal kick.

For a goal kick, the ball may be placed anywhere in that half of the goal area nearer to where the ball crossed the goal line.

OFFICIALS

There are three officials responsible for the control of a game of soccer: an appointed referee, who has primary responsibility and who controls the game on the field of play, and two linesmen, one to each touchline. The referee should have two good whistles, two reliable watches, a coin, a notebook, and a pencil. The linesmen should each have a watch, a linesman's flag, and a whistle (in case of emergency). The flags should be of contrasting colors and are usually provided by the home team. Experience has proven that orange-yellow and flame red are good colors for the flags. The linesmen should always carry their flags unfurled so that their signals will be clearly visible. The rules make no stipulation concerning the dress of the officials, but it is customary for them to wear uniforms clearly distinct from those of the players, particularly their stockings and shirts.

RULES OF PLAY

Start of Play

It is customary for the captains of the two teams to shake hands with the referee and each other before the game starts and then for the captain of the home team to toss a coin, with the captain of the visiting team giving the call. The captain who wins the toss can choose to kick off or to indicate which end of the field his or her team will defend. If the winner chooses to kick off, the other captain has the choice of ends, and vice versa. For the kickoff, the ball is placed in a stationary position in the center spot. The referee gives a signal for the kickoff, and a player from the team kicking off then takes a place kick.

Kickoff

1. Every player must remain in his or her half of the field until the ball has been played. Players of the team opposing the team kicking off must be at least 10 yards from the ball until it has been kicked off.
2. The ball must be kicked into the opponents' half of the field.
3. The ball must travel the distance of its circumference (nearly a yard) to be in play.
4. The kicker must not play the ball a second time until it has been played or touched by another player.
5. A goal cannot be scored directly from a kickoff. When rule 4 has been broken, an indirect free kick is awarded to the opposing team, but, for other infringements, the place kick is retaken.

Continuation of Play

When a goal has been scored, the game is restarted, if there is time enough left, with a kickoff by the team losing the goal. After halftime, the teams exchange ends and the game is restarted by the team that did not take the starting kickoff.

When extra time is necessary, the captains again toss for kickoff or choice of ends. In all games, the referee is empowered to:

1. Make allowances during either half of the game for time lost through accident or other causes. (The amount of time added to make up for time lost is a matter of the referee's discretion.)
2. Extend time to permit a penalty kick at or after the expiration of the regular period of time during either half of the game or in extra time.

Throw-in

When the whole of the ball passes over either touchline and is out of play on the ground or in the air, it shall be thrown in. The following points relate to the throw-in:

1. The throw-in is taken by a player of the opposing team to the player's who last touched the ball before it passed over the touchline.
2. At the moment the ball is delivered to the thrower, he or she must face the field of play.
3. At the moment the ball is delivered to the thrower, part of each of his or her feet must be on the ground, either on the touchline or on the ground outside the touchline.
4. The thrower must use both hands.
5. The thrower must deliver the ball from over his or her head.
6. The ball is in play immediately after it is thrown and passes over the touchline.
7. The thrower must not play the ball until it has been touched or played by another player.
8. If the thrower plays the ball before it has been touched or played by another player, an indirect free kick is taken by a player of the opposing team from the spot where the infringement occurred.
9. If the ball is improperly thrown in, the throw-in is taken by a player from the opposing team.
10. A goal cannot be scored directly from a throw-in.
11. A player cannot be offside from a throw-in.

Offside

The rule on offsides, stated in full, is: A player is offside if he or she is nearer his or her opponents' goal line than the ball is at the moment it is played, unless:

1. The player is in his or her own half of the field of play.
2. There are two of the opponents nearer to their own goal line than the player is.
3. The player receives the ball directly from a goal kick, a corner kick, or a throw-in, or the ball is dropped by the referee.

A player in an offside position shall not be penalized unless, in the opinion of the referee, he or she is interfering with the play or with an opponent or is seeking to gain an advantage by being in an offside position.

For an infringement of the rule, an indirect free kick shall be taken by a player of the opposing team from the place the infringement occurred. Thus, a player is *not offside* if, when the ball was last played by a player on the same team:

1. The player receiving the ball is not nearer the opponents' goal line than the ball is.
2. There are two or more opponents nearer the goal line than the player receiving the ball.
3. The player receiving the ball is in his or her own half of the field.
4. The player receives the ball directly from a throw-in, a corner kick, or a goal kick, or the ball is dropped by the referee.

FOULS AND MISCONDUCT

Players don't start a game with the intention to foul an opponent or behave in a manner that can be called misconduct against the principle of fair play. Nevertheless, the referee must be prepared to deal with infringements. When neglected, fouls can result in retaliations, which ultimately spoil the spirit of the game.

Penal Offenses

Of the nine penal offenses, eight are intentional fouls against an opponent. The ninth is primarily a technical offense; players other than the goalkeeper are not to handle the ball. It is, however, judged to be serious enough to warrant an award of a free kick outside of the penalty box or a penalty kick if handled inside the penalty box against the side committing the offense.

1. Charging an opponent violently or dangerously.
2. Charging an opponent from behind (unless he or she is intentionally obstructing).
3. Holding an opponent.
4. Striking or attempting to strike an opponent.
5. Pushing an opponent.
6. Tripping an opponent.
7. Kicking or attempting to kick an opponent.
8. Jumping at an opponent.
9. Handling the ball.

The nine offenses are penalized by the awarding of a direct free kick to the opposing team, unless the offense was committed by the defending side within the penalty area, in which case a penalty kick is awarded.

Technical Offenses

These offenses are penalized by the awarding of an indirect free kick to the opposing team:

1. Goalkeeper taking more than four steps while holding the ball.
2. Playing in a manner considered by the referee to be dangerous, such as kicking or attempting to kick the ball when it is being held by the goalkeeper.
3. Behaving in an unsportsmanlike manner.
4. Intentionally obstructing an opponent.

Appendix C

Annotated Bibliography

1. Allison, Malcolm, *Soccer for Thinkers*. London: Pelham Books, 1967.

   A useful insight into the training methods employed by a professional English club coach. Full of practical coaching tips of interest to the beginning coach.

2. Canadian Soccer Association, Publications and Audio Visual Brochures. (333 River Road, Ottawa, Ontario, Canada K1L 8B9.)

   The brochure lists all of the educational aids produced by the association, many of which have been referred to in this text (that is, *Mini Soccer* and *Indoor Soccer*).

3. Csanadi, Arpad, *Soccer,* volumes 1 and 2. Budapest: Carving Press, 1965.

   This is one of the original "bibles" of coaching textbooks. Csanadi details the Hungarian methods of skill teaching and physical conditioning and provides a wealth of information.

4. Heddergott, Karl-Heinz, *New Football Manual*. Kassel, West Germany: Limpert, 1976.

   The present director of coaching of the Deutscher Fussball-Bund outlines the teaching methods of the German coaching school in a comprehensive textbook of interest to the beginning coach.

5. Herberger, Sepp, "Modern Coaching Methods," in S. Smith and E. Batty (eds.), *International Coaching Book*. Toronto: Ryersan Press, 1966.

   The "father" of the German coaching school, Herberger outlines the principles of his coaching methods, which have stood the test of time. A useful text that provides many other insights into the methods of coaches from around the world.

6. Howell, M. L., and Marford, W. F., *Fitness Training Methods*. Toronto: Canadian Association for Health, Physical Education and Recreation, no date.

   This is the Canadian physical education textbook on fitness training methods, and although it is not specific to soccer, it provides an insight into the area of strength and muscular endurance training.

7. Hughes, Charles, *Tactics and Teamwork*. Wakefield, Great Britain: E. P. Publishing, 1973.

   A detailed insight into the principles of the modern game, this text dissects the tactics at play into easily understood concepts of interest to the teacher who wants to gain a more advanced understanding of the game.

8. Ingels, Neil B., Jr., *Coaching Youth Soccer*. Monterey, California: Page-Ficklin Publications, 1976.

   A best-seller in North America as the reference book for youth soccer coaches, the text is a valuable resource of practical drills and exercises for the beginning coach.

9. Morgan, R. E., and Adamson, G. T., *Circuit Training*. London: Bill and Sons, 1957.

   A physical education textbook that has become the model for circuit training, the original text still provides a sound basis for the development of fitness training programs.

10. Thomson, William, *Soccer Coaching Methods*. Monterey, California: Page-Ficklin Publications, 1977.

The author's first textbook outlines all of the skills and principles of play of particular interest to coaches, with a progression of drills for each of the skills.

11. Thomson, William, *Soccer School*. Ottawa: Soccer School Publications, 1977. (Box 6087, Station J, Ottawa, Ontario, Canada K2A 1T1.)

A set of individual learning programs for players and coaches, this material is organized in booklet form to provide the beginning player and teacher with an individual reference to the skills and drills for each lesson. The awards program and an explanatory film complete the Soccer School correspondence course package.

12. Wade, Allen, *The Football Association Guide to Training and Coaching*. London: Heinemann, 1967.

The official course textbook of the Football Association has become the standard reference for coaches at the higher level. The book contains a comprehensive explanation of the principles, tactics, and training methods of the modern game of soccer.

13. Worthington, Eric, *Teaching Soccer Skill*. Edinburgh: T. A. Constable, 1974.

This is an academic treatment of the science of teaching soccer skills coupled with a good practical reference for the implications of effective teaching methods on the game.

Index

Ability assessment, 3-4
Affective tasks, 6-7
Aside rules, 165. *See also* Mini soccer
Awards programs, 154

Ball control
    practice 31-33
    techniques, 29-30
Balls, 20, 22. *See also* Facilities
Bang board, 21. *See also* Facilities

Centerhalf, 106
Chipping
    practice, 63
    techniques, 61-62
Circuit training, 144-146. *See also* Conditioning;
    Weight training
Close control. *See* Dribbling
Coaching, 118-133. *See also* Teaching; Techniques
Coaching grid, 18
Coeducational groups, 15
Cognitive tasks, 6-7
Conditioning, 2-3, 133-153. *See also* Circuit training;
    Weight training
Courage (goalkeeping skill practice), 50

Defensive principles, 114-118
Dribbling
    evaluation chart, 162
    practice, 34-35, 50, 70-71, 85-87
    techniques, 33-34, 68

Equipment, 19-23
    clothing, 22-23. *See also* Facilities
Evaluation charts, 155-163
Exercise, 134

Facilities, 3, 15-19. *See also* Equipment
Fartlek (training method), 134-135
Feedback, 4

Fitness, 2. *See also* Circuit training; Conditioning;
    Exercise; Fartlek; Weight training
Forward, 108-110
Front block. *See* Tackling
Fullback, 105-106
Functional training, 104-110

Games
    indoor soccer, 17-18
    mini soccer, 16-17, 20, 57, 165-166
    small-sided games, 17-19, 56, 89-92, 132
    two-court soccer, 17-18
    warmup games, 58-61
Goalkeeping
    physical requirements for, 133-134
    practice, 43-44, 50, 77-78, 88
    techniques, 41-43, 71-76

Half volley, 62
Heading
    defensive, 54
    evaluation chart, 161
    offensive, 54-55
    practice, 45-47, 53-55, 79
    techniques, 44-45, 78, 84-85

Indoor soccer, 17-18
Instep drive. *See* Kicking and shooting
Instruction, three-phase, 4-5
Interval training, 134-141. *See also* Fartlek
    fast interval running, 138-140
    slow interval training, 135-136
    training with ball, 141

Jockeying, 132-133
Juggling, 31

Kicking and shooting, 38-40, 51-52
Kickoffs, 93-94

Kicks
    corner, 98-100
    free, 100-103
    goal, 97-98

Lesson planning, 8-9. *See also* Methods, teaching; Pre-
    teaching procedures; Teaching
Lifting the ball. *See* Chipping
Link man, 106-107

Methods, teaching
    assessment, 3-4
    organization, 2-3
    three-phase instruction, 4-5. *See also* Lesson Plan-
        ning; Preteaching procedures
Midfield player, 106-107
Mini soccer, 16-17, 20, 57, 165-166
Motivation. *See* Feedback

Objectives, behavioral, 6-7
Offensive principles, 112-114

Passing
    practice, 10-13, 26-28, 47-49, 82-84
    techniques, 24-25
Physical requirements for players, 133-134
Play
    principles of, 111-133
    systems of, 110
Positions. *See specific positions*
Practices, game-related, 88
Pressure training, 142-144
Preteaching procedures, 15. *See also* Lesson planning;
    Methods, teaching; Teaching
Psychomotor tasks, 6-7

Rebound wall, 21. *See also* Facilities
Receiving
    practice, 31-33, 52-53, 67, 79-81
    techniques, 29-30, 66
Requirements, physical, 133-134
Restarts, 92-103
Rules of soccer, 167-172
Running with ball. *See* Dribbling

Screening. *See* Dribbling
Shuttle run evaluation chart, 162
Side volley, 64
Skill teaching, 4. *See also* Task approach; Teaching;
    Technique teaching

Skills. *See* Techniques
Small-sided games, 17-19, 56, 89-92, 132
Striking techniques, 64
Sweeper, 131

Tackling
    practice, 37-38, 51, 70-71, 85-87
    techniques, 35-36, 69-70
Task approach, 1, 6-8, 10-12. *See also* Teaching
Teaching
    approach, 3
    lesson plan, 8-9
    methods, 2-5
    tasks, 1, 8, 10-12
    techniques, 4. *See also* Coaching; Evaluation charts;
        Instruction, three phase; Lesson planning;
        Preteaching procedures; Skill teaching; Task
        approach
Technique teaching, 4. *See also specific techniques*
Techniques
    ball control, 29-30
    chipping, 61-62
    dribbling, 33-34, 68
    goalkeeping, 41-43, 71-76
    heading, 44-45, 78, 84-85
    kicking and shooting, 38
    passing, 24-25
    receiving, 29-30, 66
    striking, 64
    tackling, 35-36, 69-70
    teaching, 4
    volleys, 64-65
Test, basic soccer rules, 164
Three-hundred-yard run evaluation chart, 163
Throw-in, 94-95
Training
    functional, 104-110
    pressure, 142-144. *See also* Fartlek; Interval training
Two-court soccer, 17-18

Volleys, 64-65
    evaluation chart, 158

Warmup, 148-149
    games, 58-61
Wedging, 30-33
Weight training, 146-147. *See also* Circuit training;
        Conditioning
Wing play, 107-108
WM system, 122, 124